MY BIG BIG BOOK OF
MACHINES

This a Parragon Publishing Book
First Published in 2001 Parragon, Queen Street House, 4 Queen Street, Bath BA1 1HE, UK
Copyright © Parragon 2001
ISBN 0-75256-486-2
Produced by **ticktock** *Publishing Ltd.*
Illustrations by John Alston
Photography by Roddy Paine Studios
Additional pictures supplied by: Allsport 13t. Alvey & Towers 10/11c, 32/33c, 44/45c,
70c, 106c, 107cr, 113cb. Philip Jarrett 30/31 all. Pictor 53, 55cr, 69t, 69b, 84cr, 104c, 107c.
Printed in China

MY BIG BIG BOOK OF
MACHINES

BY CHRIS OXLADE

CONTENTS

INTRODUCTION 6-9

CARS

LIMOUSINE	10-11
RACING CAR	12-13
SPORTS CAR	14-15
TAXI	16-17
4 X 4	18-19
VINTAGE CAR	20-21
SMART CAR	22-23

AIRCRAFT

HELICOPTER	24-25
BIPLANE	26-27
JET AIRLINER	28-29
FIGHTER PLANE	30-31
GLIDER	32-33
BALLOON	34-35
LIGHT AIRCRAFT	36-37

BOATS

HOVERCRAFT	38-39
TUG	40-41
SAILING DINGHY	42-43
MOTOR BOAT	44-45
FISHING BOAT	46-47
BATTLESHIP	48-49
FERRY	50-51

TRUCKS

TOW TRUCK	52-53
TRACTOR-TRAILER	54-55
TANKER	56-57
CAR CARRIER	58-59
TRUCK	60-61
GARBAGE TRUCK	62-63
CARGO VAN	64-65

●TRAINS

STEAM TRAIN	66-67
HIGH-SPEED TRAIN	68-69
COMMUTER TRAIN	70-71
TROLLEY	72-73
SHUNTING LOCOMOTIVE	74-75
MONORAIL TRAIN	76-77
MINIATURE TRAIN	78-79

●MOTORBIKES

QUAD BIKE	80-81
MOTOCROSS BIKE	82-83
SCOOTER	84-85
CUSTOM BIKE	86-87
RACING BIKE	88-89
VINTAGE MOTORBIKE	90-91
SUPERBIKE	92-93

●EMERGENCY

POLICE PATROL CAR	94-95
FIRE ENGINE	96-97
AMBULANCE	98-99
LIFEBOAT	100-101
POLICE PATROL BIKE	102-103
LADDER TRUCK	104-105
AIR-SEA RESCUE	106-107

●AT WORK

LOADER	108-109
DIGGER	110-111
MOBILE CRANE	112-113
PLOUGH	114-115
COMBINE HARVESTER	116-117
TRACTOR	118-119
FORK-LIFT TRUCK	120-121

THE MACHINE QUIZ	*122-125*
INDEX	*126-128*

This is a book all about machines – cool cars, bad bikes, large trucks, trains that travel at over 186 mph and a whole array of amazing aircraft. From lumbering brutes to outrageously fast racing machines, they are all waiting for you within these pages.

CARS

You probably see hundreds or thousands of normal cars every day. But there are lots of amazing cars that you hardly ever. They see come in all sort of shapes and sizes. There are very old, very slow cars, sleek limousines, super fast racing cars, tiny town cars and tough cars for driving through the country.

TRAINS

Trains are big machines that rumble along on railway tracks. They have cars full of passengers or wagons full of cargo. Some trains have huge locomotives that pull them along. Express trains thunder at high speed between towns and cities, while trams roll quietly through city streets. Not all trains are big. Some tiny trains are made specially for children.

Discover seven machines in each section and learn amazing facts as well as essential information about each one. Then turn to pages 122-125 for answers to those questions you are just itching to ask.

AIRCRAFT

Aircraft are big machines that fly through the air. We fly in aircraft to travel quickly around the world and to have fun in the sky. There are tiny aircraft that buzz along near the ground and monster airliners that cruise at great heights. Glider pilots swoop around in their planes while helicopter pilots can hover on the spot.

BOATS

Boats and ships are machines that move on rivers, lakes and oceans. They do dozens of different jobs, from fishing to fighting. Ferries big and small carry people, cars, buses and trucks. Sailing boats move along using the power of the wind, while speedboats with powerful engines skim across the water, bouncing through the waves.

1886

Cajensa

Emergency services such as the police, fire and ambulance service all have special machines for reaching accidents and emergencies. Some help to rescue people. Others carry sick or injured people to hospital. Some emergency services also have helicopters and boats that can rescue people from the sea or the mountains.

MOTORBIKES

If you put a motor on a bicycle you get a motorbike! There are motorbikes designed for getting around and motorbikes designed for racing. Small scooters buzz round town carrying people to work. Superbikes scream about on country roads. Most motorbikes have two wheels, but farmers have tough quad bikes that have four wheels.

TRUCKS

Trucks are the monster machines of the road. They trundle about carrying all sort of cargo, from cars to coconuts. Vans are small trucks that whiz about in busy traffic. Some trucks do special jobs. Garbage trucks gather up garbage from homes and offices, while rescue trucks rescue other vehicles that have broken down.

AT WORK

There are many big machines on wheels that don't carry anything. They are working machines. Some machines work on building sites, where they dig holes, move rubble and lift heavy materials. Farmers have machines such as tractors that help them on their farms. The machines plough fields and gather crops.

TOP QUALITY

Limousines are made by top car manufacturers such as Lincoln, Cadillac and Mercedes Benz.

LIMOUSINES NEED BIG ENGINES TO PULL THE WEIGHT OF THE CAR.

IT HAS A SMART, SHINY BODY.

LIMOUSINES HAVE DARK WINDOWS TO STOP PEOPLE LOOKING IN.

IT HAS BIG DOORS FOR GETTING IN AND OUT.

DWZ696T

STRETCHING A LIMO

A limousine is made by cutting a normal car in half and adding a bit in the middle. A stretch limousine is even longer than a normal limousine. It is like a luxury personal bus!

THE PRESIDENT OF THE U.S.A. HAS A BULLET-PROOF LIMOUSINE.

LIMOUSINE

A limousine is a monster luxury car. Pop stars and businessmen sometimes travel by limousine. They sit in the comfy seats in the back, while a driver called a chauffeur sits in the front.

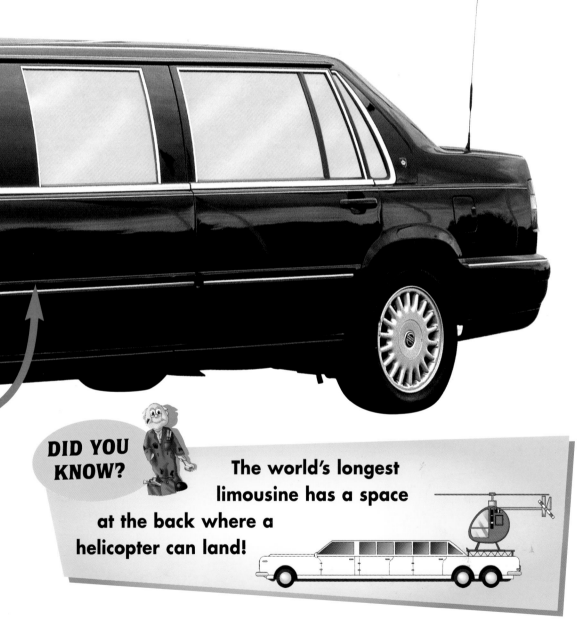

INSIDE A LIMOUSINE

Travelling in a limousine is extremely comfortable. There are big leather seats like armchairs, a table, a television and a fridge for cold drinks. There is also a telephone to let the passengers talk to the driver.

DID YOU KNOW? The world's longest limousine has a space at the back where a helicopter can land!

RACING CAR

Racing cars are high-performance cars designed for racing against each other. These single-seater vehicles can go as fast as an express train. The driver needs lots of skill to drive quickly without skidding off the track.

IN THE COCKPIT

The driver is held tightly in the cockpit by safety belts. He wears a crash helmet and fireproof clothes to protect him in case of an accident.

CAR WITH WINGS

This racing car has wings at the front and back. When the car is speeding along, air rushes over and under the wings, pushing the vehicle downwards. The tires press harder on the track, which makes them grip better.

THIS IS THE FRONT WING.

A DRAG RACER RACES ALONG A SHORT STRAIGHT TRACK.

IN THE PITS

During a race the cars stop once or twice in a garage called the pits. This is called a pit stop. Mechanics quickly change the worn-out tires for fresh tires and put in more fuel. A pit stop takes less than 10 seconds.

THE CAR HAS WING MIRRORS TO SEE VEHICLES BEHIND.

THE ENGINE IS BEHIND THE DRIVER'S COCKPIT.

www.edenbridge.co

THIS IS THE REAR WING.

THE CAR HAS WIDE, SMOOTH TIRES TO GRIP THE TRACK.

DID YOU KNOW?

The driver who wins a race sprays champagne at the other drivers for fun.

IN A HURRY

Many sports cars are capable of travelling at very high speeds. This little car was once spotted by police travelling down a motorway in England at over 155 mph.

A POWERFUL ENGINE MAKES THE CAR GO FAST.

THE WINDSCREEN STOPS WIND BLOWING IN THE DRIVER'S FACE.

THE BIG TIRES GRIP THE ROAD.

MANY SPORTS CARS USE THE SAME TECHNOLOGY AS FORMULA 1 RACING CARS.

SPORTS CAR

Sports cars are designed to travel at great speed. Their powerful acceleration means that they are very exciting to drive, but sports cars can be dangerous, and need to be handled with great care.

COSTLY TOYS

Sports cars are very expensive, sometimes costing hundreds of thousands of dollars. They are prized by the rich and famous.

THE SMOOTH FRONT HELPS THE CAR TO GO FAST.

SOFT TOP

This sports car has an automatic folding roof. When the driver presses a button on the dashboard, the roof opens or closes. When the roof is open, it folds neatly into a box behind the seats.

TAXI

If you want to get somewhere fast and you don't have a car, you might call a taxi. You tell the taxi driver where you want to get to, and off you go! When you arrive, you pay the driver for the journey.

The longest taxi journey ever was a round trip between London and Cape Town, South Africa. The fare of $57,992 was waived as the trip was for charity.

ON THE METER

A machine in the taxi called a meter works out how much you have to pay. It counts how far the taxi has travelled on your journey and how long the journey has taken. You can see the fare gradually going up as the taxi moves along.

BLACK CABS

The taxis in London are called black cabs. There are always dozens of black cabs whizzing about in London's streets. A black cab has space for five passengers in the back and space for lots of luggage next to the driver.

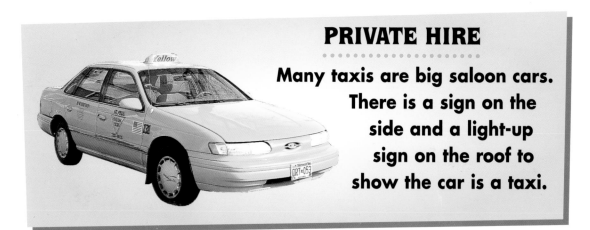

PRIVATE HIRE

Many taxis are big saloon cars. There is a sign on the side and a light-up sign on the roof to show the car is a taxi.

RICKSHAWS ARE THREE-WHEELED TAXI MOTORCYCLES USED IN PARTS OF ASIA.

THIS SIGN LIGHTS UP WHEN THE TAXI IS FREE.

THE WIDE DOORS LET PEOPLE IN AND OUT EASILY.

THE DOORS LOCK TO STOP PEOPLE JUMPING OUT WHEN THE TAXI IS MOVING.

THESE BIG BUMPERS PROTECT THE TAXI FROM BUMPS.

W238 WGH

ALL THE TAXIS IN NEW YORK ARE BRIGHT YELLOW.

A monster truck is a pick-up truck with enormous wheels. It can squash other cars flat!

DID YOU KNOW?

FOUR-WHEEL DRIVE

In a 4 x 4 car, all four wheels turn round. This means that the car can go almost anywhere, however terrible the conditions. It can travel up steep hills and through mud or snow without getting stuck.

4 X 4'S HAVE BIG, CHUNKY TIRES.

4 X 4 CARS CAN DRIVE UP HILLS AS STEEP AS STAIRS.

4 X 4

4x 4 is short for 'four by four'. 4 x 4 cars are good at going up and down steep hills and along bumpy roads in the countryside. They have big chunky tires that prevent the car getting stuck in mud.

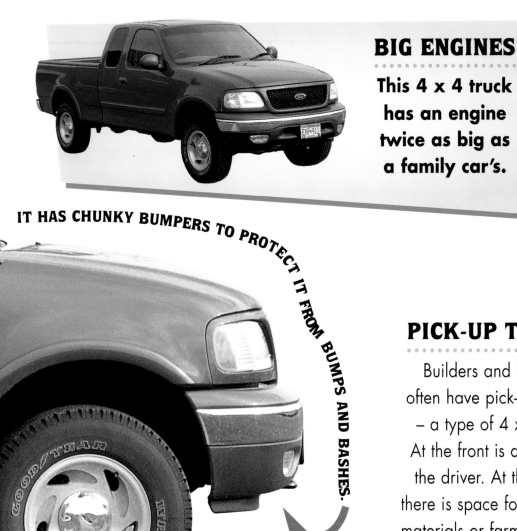

BIG ENGINES

This 4 x 4 truck has an engine twice as big as a family car's.

IT HAS CHUNKY BUMPERS TO PROTECT IT FROM BUMPS AND BASHES.

PICK-UP TRUCK

Builders and farmers often have pick-up trucks – a type of 4 x 4 car. At the front is a cab for the driver. At the back there is space for building materials or farm animals.

THE FIRST 4 X 4 CAR WAS THE FAMOUS JEEP.

VINTAGE CAR

A vintage car is a very old car. While modern cars are often factory-made, and fashioned out of one big piece of metal, vintage cars were often put together in several pieces by hand. Very old vintage cars look like horse-drawn carriages.

THE PRICE IS RIGHT

The small vintage car on the right is an Austin Seven. It was made in the 1920s. It was one of the first cars that was cheap enough for ordinary people to buy.

STARTER HANDLE

The driver turns a handle to start the car's engine. It is very hard work!

CAR COLLECTORS

Vintage cars are very valuable. Some people collect them. Collectors keep their cars clean and shiny and display them at vintage car shows. They also dress in old clothes and drive their cars at vintage car rallies.

THE MOST FAMOUS VINTAGE CAR IS THE MODEL-T FORD.

The Austin Seven was so small that people said it looked like a toy car.

THE HEAD LAMPS ARE ON STICKS.

THE WHEELS HAVE WIRE SPOKES.

THE RADIATOR COOLS THE ENGINE.

AZ 5 80

THE FIRST EVER CAR WAS DRIVEN BY A HUGE STEAM ENGINE!

On a Smart car the colored panels are easy to take off and change for a different color.

THE GLASS ROOF LETS LIGHT INTO THE CAR.

SMART CARS HAVE STRONG METAL FRAMES.

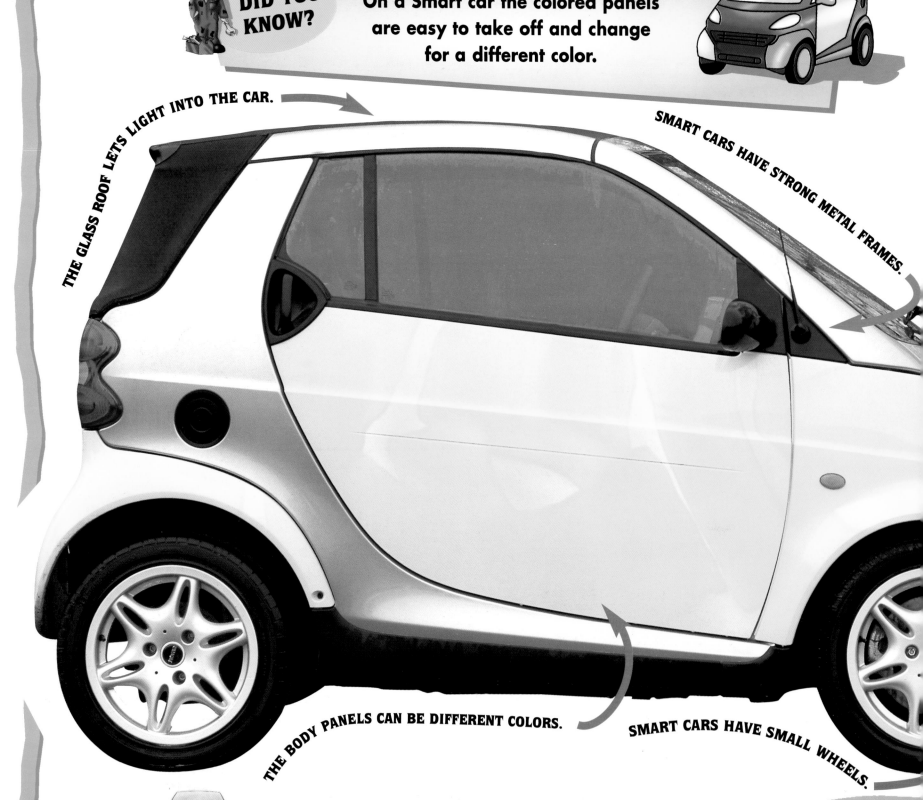

THE BODY PANELS CAN BE DIFFERENT COLORS.

SMART CARS HAVE SMALL WHEELS.

SOME SMALL TOWN CARS HAVE ELECTRIC MOTORS INSTEAD OF ENGINES.

SMART CAR

A Smart car is a tiny car for two people. It can squeeze into small parking spaces and turn very sharp corners. This makes it good for driving in busy towns and cities.

SMART PARTS

Smart cars are put together very cleverly. They have a strong metal frame called a safety cell that protects the driver and passenger in case of an accident. Most of its parts are recyclable.

UNDER THE SEATS

The Smart car's engine is at the back under the seats. It is a 600 cc engine, which is half the size of the engine in a family car. There are only three gears. Its top speed is just 84 mph.

DID YOU KNOW?

Although the bodies of smart cars are made entirely from plastic, they are one of the strongest and safest small cars in the world.

SMART CARS ARE JUST OVER SIX AND A HALF FEET LONG.

HELICOPTER

A helicopter is an aircraft that can hover in the air. A helicopter does not have wings. Instead it has a set of thin blades called a rotor. The rotor spins very fast, lifting the helicopter into the air.

SKIDS AND WHEELS

This helicopter lands on metal feet called skids. Larger helicopters have wheels so that they can roll along.

HELICOPTER JOBS

Helicopters can take off and land in a small space. They are used in places where there is no space to build runways for normal aircraft, such as in the mountains or in the jungle. They are also used for rescuing people from the sea.

FLYING A HELICOPTER

Flying a helicopter is quite tricky. A pilot uses the controls in the cockpit to make the helicopter go up or down, forwards or backwards, left or right, or turn round. The small rotor on the tail stops the fuselage spinning round instead of the rotor.

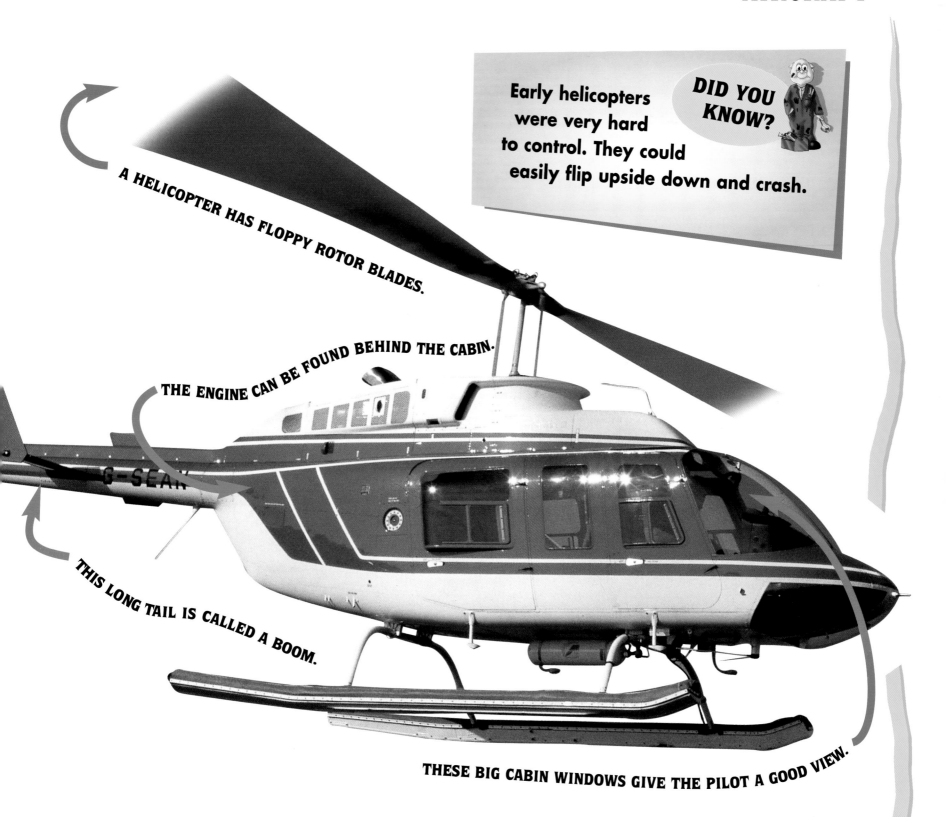

DID YOU KNOW?

Early helicopters were very hard to control. They could easily flip upside down and crash.

A HELICOPTER HAS FLOPPY ROTOR BLADES.

THE ENGINE CAN BE FOUND BEHIND THE CABIN.

THIS LONG TAIL IS CALLED A BOOM.

THESE BIG CABIN WINDOWS GIVE THE PILOT A GOOD VIEW.

SOME HELICOPTERS HAVE FLOATS FOR LANDING ON WATER.

BIPLANE PARTS

The part of a biplane where the pilot sits is called the fuselage. The engine is at the front of the fuselage. The two pairs of wings are held together with rods and wires. The aircraft must be very strong in order to perform high-speed stunts.

DID YOU KNOW?

In 1904 a pilot built an aircraft which had an amazing 20 pairs of wings. It didn't fly!

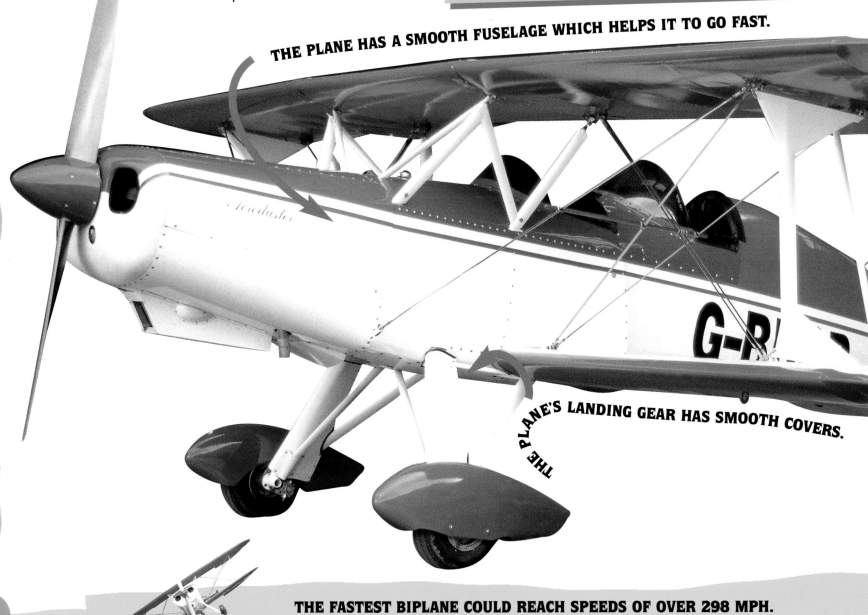

THE PLANE HAS A SMOOTH FUSELAGE WHICH HELPS IT TO GO FAST.

THE PLANE'S LANDING GEAR HAS SMOOTH COVERS.

THE FASTEST BIPLANE COULD REACH SPEEDS OF OVER 298 MPH.

BIPLANE

A biplane is an aircraft with two pairs of wings. Most aircraft only have one pair of wings. Pilots of biplanes regularly perform incredible stunts in the air called aerobatics.

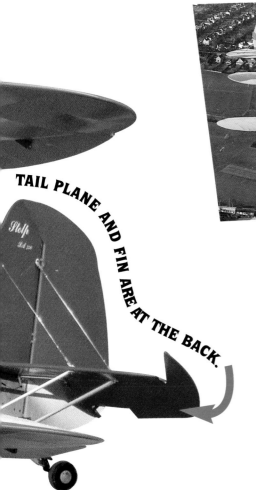

TAIL PLANE AND FIN ARE AT THE BACK.

LOOPING THE LOOP

In aerobatics pilots do amazing stunts. They climb steeply, fly upside down and dive down again. This is called looping the loop. They also do spins and rolls. The pilot wears a belt to stop him from falling out when the aircraft is upside down.

LOTS OF POWER

An aerobatics biplane has a very powerful engine. The engine turns a big propeller, which pulls the biplane along.

THE SMALLEST BIPLANE EVER HAD A WINGSPAN OF UNDER SIX AND A HALF FEET.

JET AIRLINER

An airliner is an aircraft that carries passengers. Large airliners have powerful jet engines that push them through the air. The biggest airliners can carry more than 500 people. Small airliners carry about 50 people.

READY TO LAND

As an airliner approaches the runway it slows down and unfolds its landing gear.

THE PILOTS SIT IN THE COCKPIT.

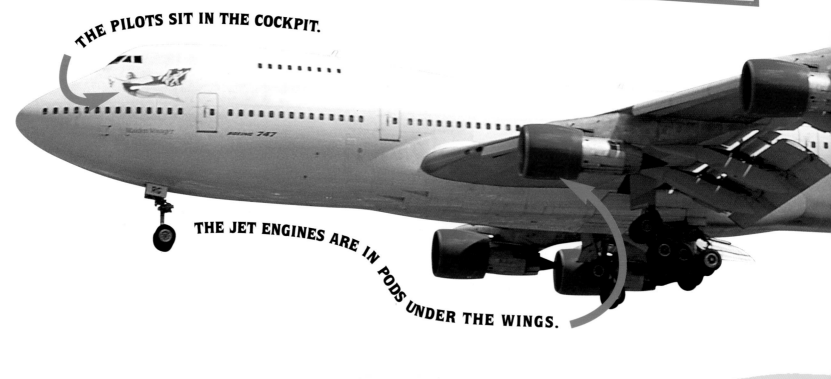

THE JET ENGINES ARE IN PODS UNDER THE WINGS.

PLANS HAVE BEEN CONFIRMED FOR A DOUBLE-DECKER AIRLINER.

A LONG HAUL

Large airliners like the Boeing 747 can fly halfway round the world without stopping. They stay in the air for more than 12 hours. The Boeing 747 has four huge jet engines, and its wings are as wide as a soccer pitch.

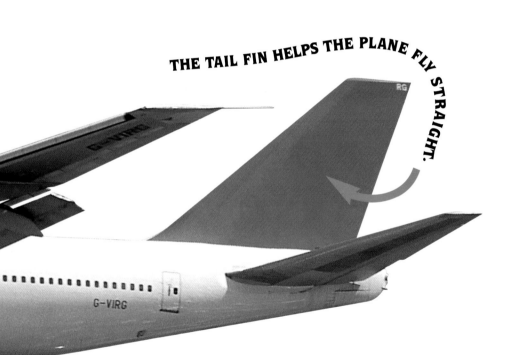

THE TAIL FIN HELPS THE PLANE FLY STRAIGHT.

DID YOU KNOW?

The first airliners flew around 1920. They were built out of old bombers from World War One.

INSIDE THE FUSELAGE

The airliner's fuselage is a big metal tube. Inside the fuselage are seats for the passengers, galleys for making food and drink, and toilets. Under the floor is the baggage hold where the passenger's baggage is stored. Animals also travel in the baggage hold.

A BOEING 747 ONCE CARRIED MORE THAN 1,000 PEOPLE.

FLYING FAST

Fighter planes have big, powerful jet engines. They fly two or three times faster than jet airliners. They can also climb and dive steeply, and turn very sharp corners. This helps them to attack enemy aircraft and to keep out of trouble themselves.

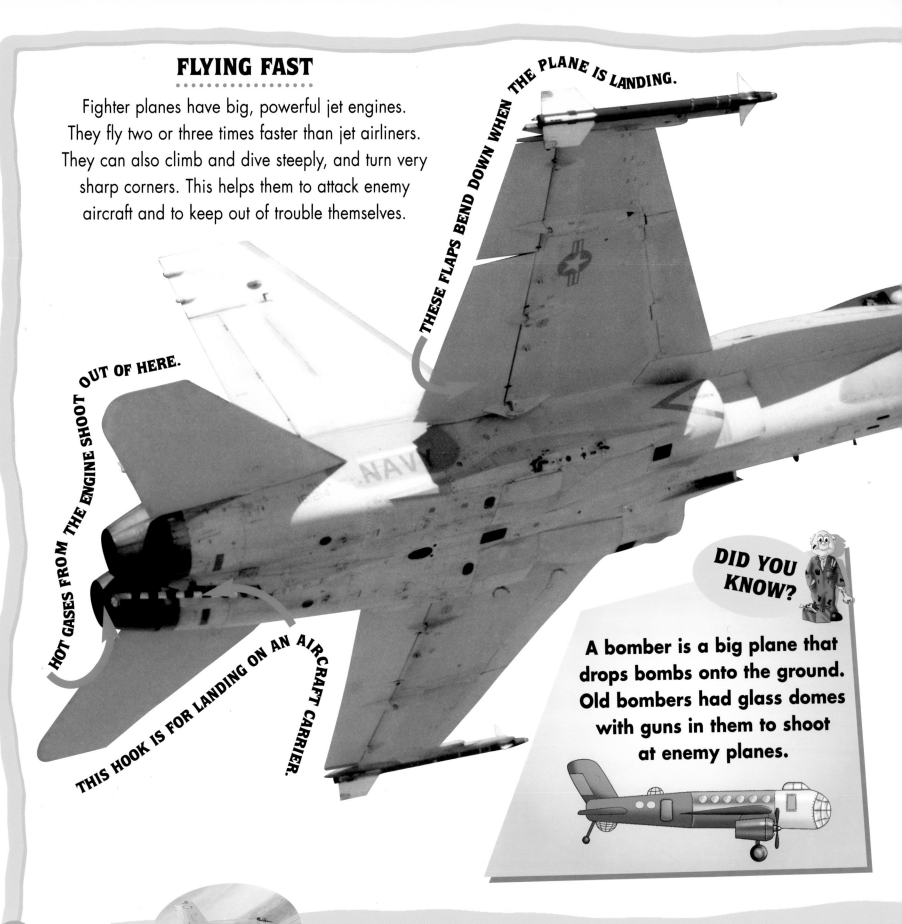

THESE FLAPS BEND DOWN WHEN THE PLANE IS LANDING.

HOT GASES FROM THE ENGINE SHOOT OUT OF HERE.

THIS HOOK IS FOR LANDING ON AN AIRCRAFT CARRIER.

DID YOU KNOW?

A bomber is a big plane that drops bombs onto the ground. Old bombers had glass domes with guns in them to shoot at enemy planes.

IF A FIGHTER PLANE IS HIT, THE PILOT CAN ESCAPE IN AN EJECTOR SEAT.

FIGHTER PLANE

A fighter plane zooms around the sky at tremendous speed. Its job is to shoot down enemy planes with its guns, rockets and missiles. When fighter planes fight each other, the battle is called a dogfight.

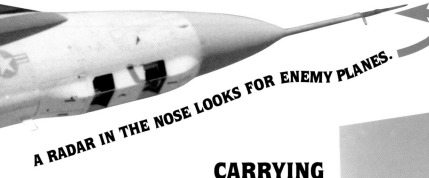

A RADAR IN THE NOSE LOOKS FOR ENEMY PLANES.

CARRYING WEAPONS

Missiles are attached to the bottom of the fighter plane's wings. The plane's computer spots enemy planes and helps the pilot to aim the missiles. After a missile is fired, it follows the enemy plane until it catches it or the plane escapes.

FIGHTER BOMBERS

Some fighter planes attack things on the ground as well as other aircraft. They are called fighter bombers. They dive towards the ground, release their bombs then climb away again.

THE FASTEST FIGHTERS CAN FLY AT 2,170 MPH.

GLIDER

On summer days you often see gliders swooping slowly and quietly around the sky. A glider is a plane without an engine. People fly gliders for fun and in competitions to see who can fly the farthest.

TRICKS AND TECHNIQUES

In order to stay up in the sky, glider pilots try to find warm air flowing upwards. This keeps the glider in the sky for longer. When coming in to land, the pilot must get it right first time, because unlike with a jet plane, there is no chance of another try!

THE BIG GLASS COCKPIT GIVES THE PILOT A GOOD VIEW.

THE SMALL WHEEL IS FOR TAKE-OFF AND LANDING.

IN THE COCKPIT

The pilot steers using a stick and two foot pedals. Seat belts are needed to hold the pilot in when the glider flies upside down.

A PARAGLIDER IS A CROSS BETWEEN A GLIDER AND A PARACHUTE.

GETTING INTO THE AIR

A glider can't take off on its own. It is towed along a runway by a car or another aircraft using a towing rope. When it is going fast enough, it takes off and climbs into the sky. Then the pilot lets go of the towing rope.

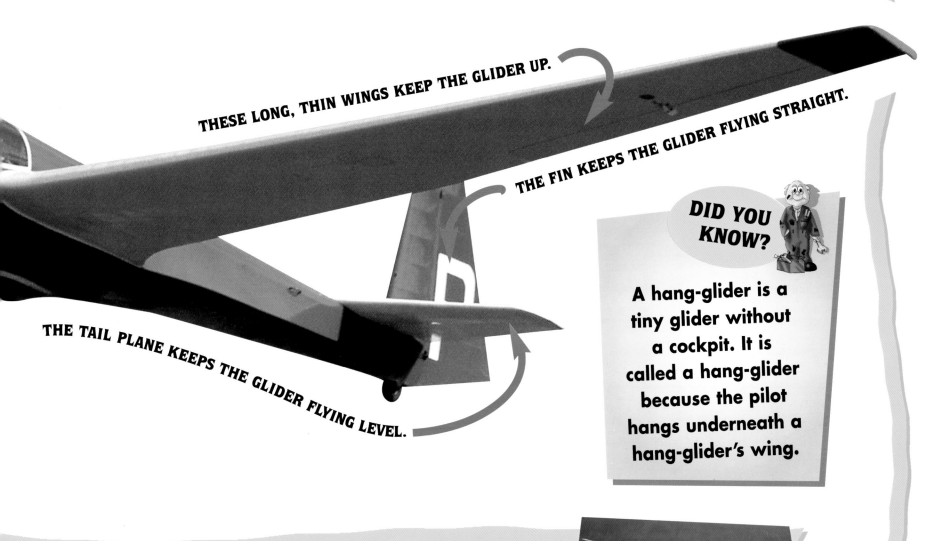

THESE LONG, THIN WINGS KEEP THE GLIDER UP.

THE FIN KEEPS THE GLIDER FLYING STRAIGHT.

THE TAIL PLANE KEEPS THE GLIDER FLYING LEVEL.

DID YOU KNOW?

A hang-glider is a tiny glider without a cockpit. It is called a hang-glider because the pilot hangs underneath a hang-glider's wing.

THE FIRST PLANES EVER TO FLY WERE GLIDERS.

BAG OF AIR

The balloon that holds the hot air is called an envelope. It is made of strips of plastic fabric stitched together along the edges. When the envelope is full of hot air it is very light. It floats upwards, carrying the basket with it.

STRONG ROPES SUPPORT THE BALLOON'S BASKET.

THIS BASKET HOLDS THE PASSENGERS.

THESE PANELS ARE MADE OF FABRIC.

POWERING UP

Huge gas burners heat the air inside the balloon to make it hot and light. They make a noisy roar.

IN 1988, A HOT-AIR BALLOON REACHED A HEIGHT OF NEARLY 65,800 FEET!

BALLOON

A hot-air balloon is an aircraft that floats into the air. Passengers travel in a basket that hangs underneath the balloon. People enjoy floating slowly and quietly over the countryside in balloons.

THIS HOLE LETS OUT THE HOT AIR.

FLYING A BALLOON

A hot-air balloon goes where the wind blows it. The pilot cannot steer. To go up, the pilot lights a gas burner to heat up the air in the balloon. To go down, the pilot lets some hot air out of the balloon through a hole in the top.

The first living things to fly in a hot-air balloon were a sheep, a rooster and a duck!

DID YOU KNOW?

AN AIRSHIP IS LIKE A BALLOON WITH POINTED ENDS AND AN ENGINE.

35

LIGHT AIRCRAFT

There are many kinds of small aircraft. Some are small airliners, which carry about 10 passengers. Other small aircraft are private jets, often owned by pop stars, sports stars and business people.

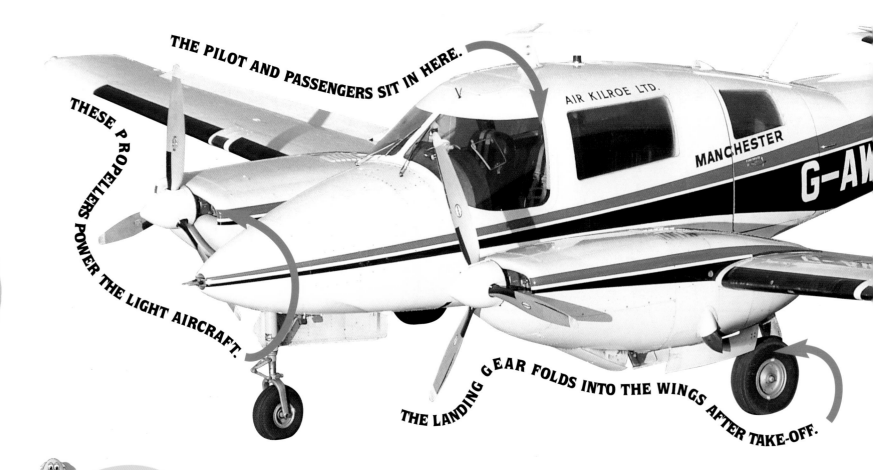

THE PILOT AND PASSENGERS SIT IN HERE.

THESE PROPELLERS POWER THE LIGHT AIRCRAFT.

THE LANDING GEAR FOLDS INTO THE WINGS AFTER TAKE-OFF.

AIR KILROE LTD.

MANCHESTER

G-AW

DID YOU KNOW? The smallest aircraft ever was called Bumble Bee Two. It was only 9 feet long!

LITTLE AIRLINER

This small airliner has seats for 10 passengers and their luggage. It is used for short trips between towns and cities. It has two engines called turboprop engines. They are jet engines that turn propellers. Two pilots sit in the cockpit.

IN AUSTRALIA, A LIGHT AIRCRAFT ONCE MADE 297 TAKE-OFFS AND LANDINGS IN JUST ONE DAY.

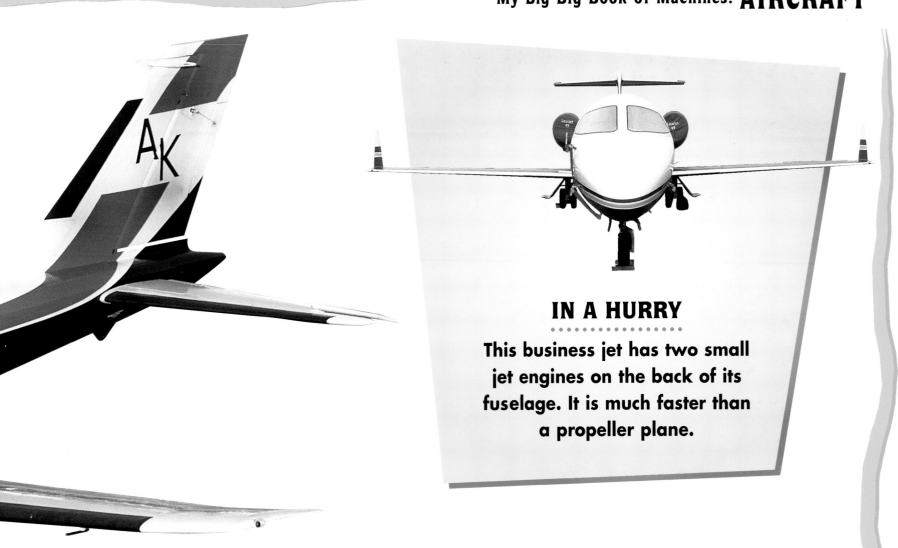

IN A HURRY

This business jet has two small jet engines on the back of its fuselage. It is much faster than a propeller plane.

PROPELLER AIRLINER

A small aircraft with a few seats and a propeller engine is called a light aircraft. Light aircraft are used for short journeys, for fun flying and for learning to fly. They have engines like the engine in a car.

If a hovercraft's fan breaks down its cushion of air goes flat. It drops into the water but does not sink.

PASSENGER FERRY

Passengers, cars and luggage are loaded onto a hovercaft when it is flat on the ground. When the vessel is ready to start its journey, the rubber skirt around the craft inflates, and it is time to go!

THE CREW STEERS THE HOVERCRAFT FROM THE BRIDGE.

THE RUBBER SKIRT KEEPS THE AIR IN.

hoverspeed.com

SOME PEOPLE BUILD AND RACE SMALL HOVERCRAFT.

HOVERCRAFT

A hovercraft hovers just above the water on a cushion of air. It skims quickly across the surface. A hovercraft can go where a normal boat can't. It can go across shallow water and even on land.

AIR IN ITS SKIRT

Inside a hovercraft is a huge fan. It sucks air in and blows it under the hovercraft. This makes a cushion of air underneath the hovercraft. A strong rubber skirt stops the air escaping. Two huge propellers blow air backwards. This makes the hovercraft zoom forwards.

hoverspeed.com

HYDROFOIL

Hydrofoils have replaced hovercrafts in many places. They have underwater wings called foils that lift the boat out of the sea, allowing it to glide above the water.

THE BIGGEST HOVERCRAFT CAN CARRY 400 PASSENGERS AND 60 CARS.

39

TUG

Tugs are sturdy working boats with powerful engines. Their job is to pull big ships like tankers in and out of ports and harbors. Tugs also rescue ships that have broken down at sea.

TUGS IN WAITING

Salvage tugs are the monsters of the tug world. A salvage tug can pull a giant supertanker on its own. Salvage tugs sit out at sea waiting for ships to break down. The first tug that reaches a ship gets the job of rescuing it.

DID YOU KNOW?

Every big port has its own fire-fighting tug. The tug sucks up sea water and sprays it over a burning ship or building.

TUGS HAVE A BIG FLAT DECK TO CARRY EQUIPMENT.

SOME TUGS CARRY FOOD, FUEL AND EQUIPMENT TO DRILLING RIGS AT SEA.

PULLING AND PUSHING

A tug pulls ships with a thick, strong rope. The tug's crew put the rope round a big hook on the tug's deck. The tug takes the strain and slowly the ship starts to move. Tugs also nudge ships about by pushing with their bows.

BREAKING WAVES

Tugs often go to sea in nasty weather. They have strong, high bows at the front that break through the really big waves.

THE BRIDGE IS HIGH UP TO GIVE A GOOD VIEW.

FOXBAY

THE RUBBER EDGE AROUND THE DECKS PROTECTS AGAINST BUMPS.

A BIG SALVAGE TUG CAN TOW AN OIL RIG AS TALL AS A SKYSCRAPER.

DID YOU KNOW?

Every year in Australia, sailors race each other in dinghies made from bath tubs!

RODS CALLED BATTENS MAKE THE SAIL STIFF.

1886

THE MAST IS MADE OF STRONG METAL.

TWO HULLS

A catamaran dinghy has two hulls side by side. Catamarans are very fast but they are tricky to sail. The crew needs lots of skill and quick reactions. When its windy, the boat tips up. One of the hulls lifts out of the water.

WIRES STOP THE MAST FALLING DOWN.

Cajensa

THE SHARP BOWS CUT THROUGH THE WATER.

THE FIRST PERSON TO SAIL ROUND THE WORLD ON HIS OWN COULD NOT SWIM.

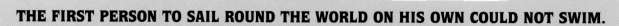

SAILING DINGHY

Flying along in a sailing dinghy is exciting and fun. The wind pushes on the sails, making the dinghy move forwards. In a strong wind a dinghy skims across the water at high speed.

HANGING OUT

One person (called the helmsman) steers the boat. In strong winds the other person often has to hang out over the water to stop the dinghy tipping over. Sometimes a dinghy does tip over. This is called capsizing.

DOWN BELOW

The keel is a heavy weight that hangs under a yacht to stop it being blown over.

MOTOR BOAT

If you want to get somewhere in a hurry you need a motor boat. They are fast, tough boats ideal for travelling at speed. Motor boats range from partly inflatable dinghies to powerboats.

GETTING TO GRIPS

Turning the steering wheel makes the outboard motor swing left or right. This makes the boat turn.

ENGINE ON THE BACK

Just like sports cars, powerboats are driven by engines. These are called either inboard or outboard motors. Outboard motors hang over the back of the boat. Because powerboats go so fast, the ride is often quite bumpy for any passengers on board!

THE OUTBOARD MOTOR POWERS THE POWERBOAT.

ARMIES AND NAVIES OFTEN USE MOTORIZED DINGHIES FOR SECRET LANDINGS.

ANYWHERE, ANYHOW

This tiny boat has a rubber hull that is filled with air. Boats like these are often used for rescues near the shore because they are quick to launch and can travel in shallow water.

If a big wave fills the dinghy with water the craft still floats. The rubber tube works like a beach ball.

DID YOU KNOW?

THE CABIN KEEPS THE CREW WARM AND DRY.

THE FASTEST SPEEDBOAT IN THE WORLD COULD TRAVEL THE LENGTH OF THE NILE IN 13 HOURS.

45

DID YOU KNOW?

The holes in fishing nets must be large enough to let young fish escape. Only adult fish are trapped.

A FRAME LIFTS NETS ONTO THE DECK.

THESE LIGHTS SHOW OTHER SHIPS WHERE THE BOAT IS AT NIGHT.

THE SCUPPERS LET WATER DRAIN OFF THE DECK.

THE HIGH BOWS BREAK THROUGH BIG WAVES.

RX59 Our Lady

A FACTORY FISHING SHIP HAS FREEZERS WHERE FISH ARE STORED.

FISHING BOAT

Every day thousands of fishermen go out to sea in their fishing boats. They take huge nets to catch fish. They even go when the wind is strong and the waves are huge, so fishermens' boats need to be very sturdy.

FISHING NETS

Fishermen throw their nets into the water. The boat moves along and the net scoops up lots of fish. Then the fishermen haul the nets back in with machinery. They open the nets and the fish plop onto the boat's deck.

BOATS OF PLANKS

Small fishing boats are made of wood. Inside is a strong wooden frame like a skeleton. On the outside are overlapping planks. The wheelhouse keeps the crew dry and warm. These fishing boats are called inshore fishing boats because they stay near the coast.

POTS AND FLAGS

Some fishermen fish for lobsters and crabs. They drop traps into the sea and return later to see what they have caught. Each trap has a flag to show where it is.

FISHING BOATS HAVE SONAR MACHINES THAT SHOW WHERE FISH ARE.

BATTLESHIP

A battleship is a fast fighting ship. It has weapons to attack other warships and submarines, and the technology to defend itself. Hundreds of sailors live and work on the ship.

SEA MONSTERS

Some battleships are so large they need a crew of 6,000 to go to sea, and weigh more than 1,000 jumbo jets.

A TIGHT SQUEEZE

On a battleship, the sailors live in cabins inside the hull. They don't have much space. On some ships they have to share beds! Their food is made in kitchens called galleys. In the middle of the ship is a room called the operations room. This is where sailors control the weapons.

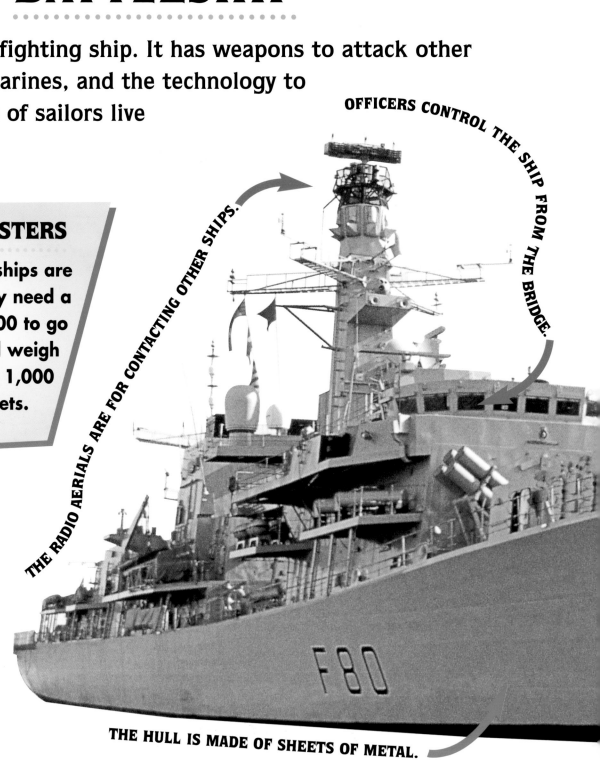

OFFICERS CONTROL THE SHIP FROM THE BRIDGE.

THE RADIO AERIALS ARE FOR CONTACTING OTHER SHIPS.

THE HULL IS MADE OF SHEETS OF METAL.

F80

BATTLESHIPS HAVE SPACE ON BOARD FOR A HELICOPTER TO LAND.

WARSHIP WEAPONS

A battleship has guns, missiles and torpedoes. These weapons are very clever. The guns aim themselves automatically. They can even aim when the ship is rolling about in the waves. The missiles fly automatically, too. They are called guided missiles.

ANCHORS GRIP THE SEA BED WHEN SHIP STOPS.

DID YOU KNOW?

Two hundred years ago battleships had sails instead of engines, and canons instead of guns. They were made of wood.

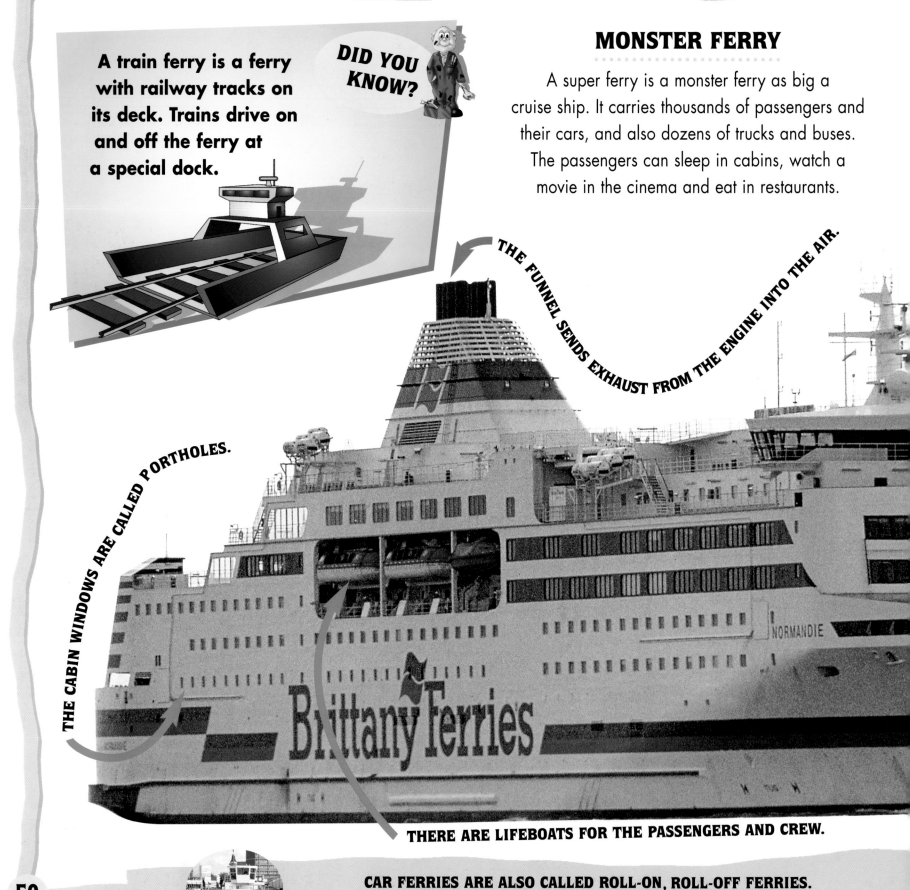

A train ferry is a ferry with railway tracks on its deck. Trains drive on and off the ferry at a special dock.

DID YOU KNOW?

MONSTER FERRY

A super ferry is a monster ferry as big a cruise ship. It carries thousands of passengers and their cars, and also dozens of trucks and buses. The passengers can sleep in cabins, watch a movie in the cinema and eat in restaurants.

THE FUNNEL SENDS EXHAUST FROM THE ENGINE INTO THE AIR.

THE CABIN WINDOWS ARE CALLED PORTHOLES.

NORMANDIE

Brittany Ferries

THERE ARE LIFEBOATS FOR THE PASSENGERS AND CREW.

CAR FERRIES ARE ALSO CALLED ROLL-ON, ROLL-OFF FERRIES.

FERRY

A ferry is a ship that carries people, cars, buses and trucks across rivers, lakes and seas. For people in remote places, taking a ferry is sometimes the only way to get to work or to the shops.

CAPTAIN'S CABIN

The ferry's bridge is high up at the front. From here the captain can easily guide the ferry into port.

SPEEDY TURN ROUND

Ferries hardly ever stop. Some go backwards and forwards all day and all night. These roll-on, roll-off craft try to turn round as fast as possible. Ferries have large doors at each end, and ramps so that vehicles can drive on and off quickly.

TOW TRUCK

I f your car has broken down you might need to be rescued by a mechanic in a tow truck. A tow truck carries broken-down vehicles to a garage where they can be fixed.

COLLECTING A CAR

To pick up a car, the driver of a tow truck parks in front of the vehicle. Then he tips the flat back up to make a ramp. A machine called a winch pulls the car up the ramp with a strong wire rope. Then the back tips back level again.

TYING ON

After a car is loaded onto the back of a tow truck, the driver ties the car's wheels down to stop the car rolling off accidentally.

THE POWERFUL DIESEL ENGINE LIES UNDER THE BONNET.

TOW TRUCKS ARE ALSO CALLED PICK-UP TRUCKS OR RECOVERY TRUCKS.

BUS CARRIER

You need a monster tow truck to rescue a bus. It can't lift the bus onto its back, so it picks up the bus's front wheels and pulls it along. It has a huge engine to pull the heavy bus. Tow trucks rescue cargo trucks, too.

THIS IS THE EXHAUST PIPE FROM THE ENGINE.

FOUR BIG BACK WHEELS TAKE THE WEIGHT OF THE LOAD.

THERE IS SPACE FOR THE CAR'S DRIVER AND PASSENGERS IN THE TRUCK'S CAB.

Truck drivers have citizen's band (CB) radios. They warn each other about obstructions jams or bad weather.

DID YOU KNOW?

ALL CHANGE

The front part of an tractor-trailer is called a tractor unit. The back part is called a trailer. The two halves can be separated so that the tractor can pull different trailers. At the back of the cab is a huge hook that connects to the trailer.

THE SMOOTH CAB TOP LETS AIR FLOW OVER THE TRAILER.

THIS TRAILER HAS CURTAIN SIDES.

DEREK LINCH

U·K· NETHERLANDS

95 XF

DAF

ROMNEY MARSH   AMSTELDEEN
KENT U.K.   NETHERLANDS

BJ·HR·24

Derek Li

U.K. & EUR
ROMNEY MARS

LARGE MIRRORS HELP THE DRIVER SEE BEHIND.

A ROAD TRAIN IS A TRACTOR-TRAILER WITH THREE TRAILERS.

TRACTOR-TRAILER

A tractor-trailer is a monster truck with two halves. In the middle is a hinge that lets the truck bend. Tractor-trailers carry all sorts of cargo, from ice cream to cows.

MEGA ENGINES

Tractor-trailers have massive diesel engines. The engines are 10 times as powerful as the engine in a family car. The driver has up to 15 gears to choose from. Some gears are for lumbering slowly up steep hills. Others are for cruising along the highway.

THE MANY WHEELS MEAN THE HEAVY LOAD IS SHARED OUT.

COMFY CABS

Tractor-trailers have big cabs. Behind the seats is a bed where the driver sleeps. There is often a shower and toilet too.

TANKER

If you need to move lots of liquid you need a tanker truck. A tanker truck is a truck with a huge tank on its back. Thousands of tankers are needed to keep petrol stations supplied with fuel for car drivers to buy.

FILLING AND EMPTYING

The liquid goes in the top and out of the bottom. There are holes in the top where the liquid is poured in. At the bottom are holes where the liquid comes out again. The liquid can be pumped along a rubber pipe stored behind the driver's cab.

WARNING SIGNS

Tankers have bright signs that show what's inside. The sign on the bottom right of this tanker means that it is carrying a flammable liquid.

PRESSURE TANK

Some tankers carry liquids that turn into gas when they come out of the tank. The gas must be squeezed tightly into the tank to make it into liquid. The tank must be very, very strong, otherwise it would explode!

TANKERS CARRY WATER WHEN THERE IS A DROUGHT.

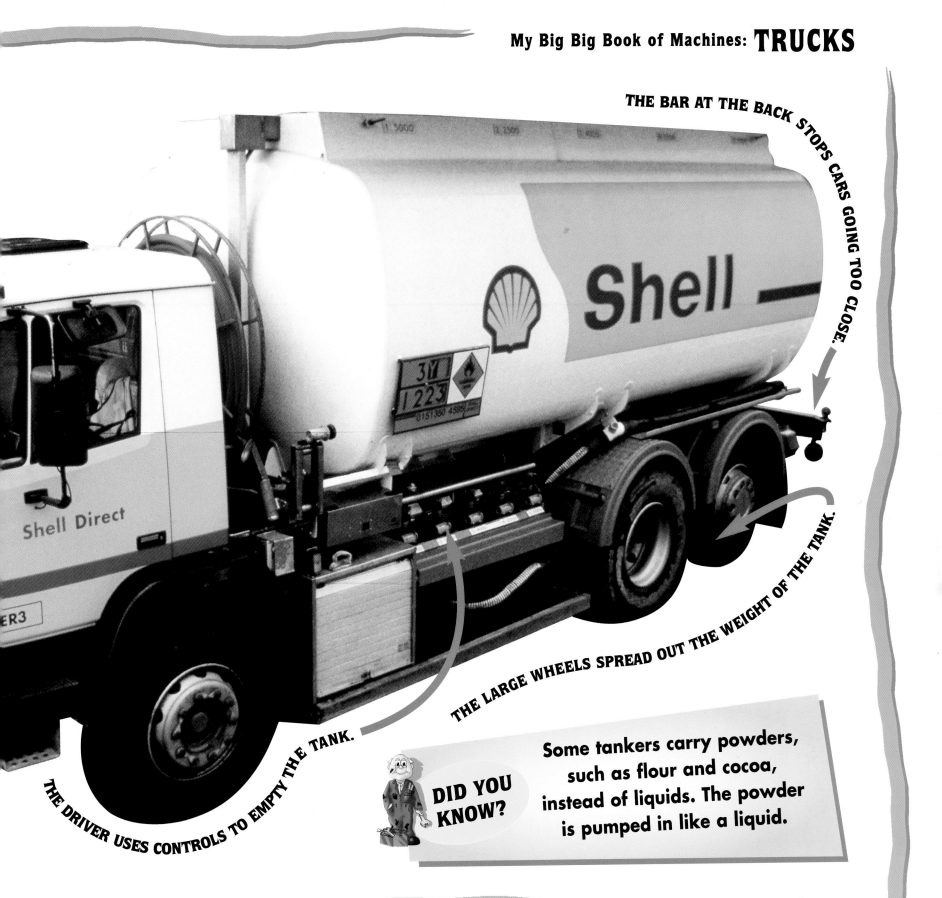

THE BAR AT THE BACK STOPS CARS GOING TOO CLOSE.

Shell

Shell Direct

3 Y
1 223
0151350 4585

THE LARGE WHEELS SPREAD OUT THE WEIGHT OF THE TANK.

THE DRIVER USES CONTROLS TO EMPTY THE TANK.

DID YOU KNOW?

Some tankers carry powders, such as flour and cocoa, instead of liquids. The powder is pumped in like a liquid.

DID YOU KNOW?

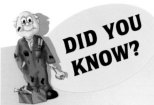

Trucks are delivered from a factory on other trucks. A truck sitting on a truck is a strange sight!

LOADING RAMPS

The top deck of a car carrier is made up of ramps. Inside the deck supports are hydraulic rams. They lower the back of the deck to make a ramp. The cars drive onto the ramp. Then the rams lift the ramp up again.

THE DRIVER CLIMBS A LADDER TO GET TO THE TOP DECK.

THIS HINGE LETS THE TRUCK GO ROUND CORNERS.

SOME TRUCKS CARRY TRAINS INSTEAD OF CARS.

CAR CARRIER

A car carrier is a truck that carries cars from a factory to the showrooms where people buy the cars. A car carrier is cleverly designed so that as many cars as possible can fit on. The one in the main picture can carry up to nine cars.

A TRICKY PUZZLE

Loading and unloading a car carrier is like doing a puzzle. The cars must be loaded and unloaded in the right order or they will not all fit on. The cars on the top deck are loaded first and unloaded last.

SPACE SAVER

Not even the space over the driver's cab is wasted. The front car is loaded first and unloaded last.

HUGE BOATS ARE USED TO CARRY MILLIONS OF CARS AROUND THE WORLD EVERY YEAR.

59

DIFFERENT SHAPES

There are dozens of different kinds of trucks. Ones like this have a big box on the back to keep the cargo dry. Some have a flat back with no body. Some trucks are made into mobile cranes, fire engines, garbage trucks and tankers.

TRUCK

A truck does not bend in the middle like a tracter-trailor. It has a cab at the front and space for cargo at the back. Trucks carry all sorts of cargo, from ice cream to computers.

CEARNS & BROWN

STRONG WHEELS ARE NEEDED TO CARRY THE HEAVY CARGO.

SOME TRUCKS HAVE A LIFT ON THE BACK FOR LOADING AND UNLOADING.

EASY ACCESS

This truck has curtain sides made of strong, waterproof plastic. The sides of the body pull back like curtains for loading and unloading.

A WIND DEFLECTOR MAKES AIR FLOW SMOOTHLY OVER THE BODY.

THESE SIDE DOORS OPEN TO LOAD THE FRONT OF THE BODY.

STAY FRESH

Many trucks are used to take food to supermarkets. Some have refrigerated units in the back to ensure produce stays fresh.

SOME TRUCKS HAVE A BODY LIKE A HUGE FRIDGE FOR CARRYING FROZEN FOODS.

GARBAGE CRUSHER

On the back of the truck's body is a powerful crushing machine. The crusher squashes the garbage down and squeezes it back into the truck's body.

CRUSHER CONTROLS

There are controls on the back for working the truck. There are buttons for lifting and tipping cans into the crusher, and buttons for making the crusher crush. There are also buttons for tipping up the body to make the garbage come out.

THE STRONG PIPES CARRY LIQUID TO WORK THE RAMS.

THESE CONTROLS MAKE THE BODY TIP UP.

THESE STEPS ARE USED FOR GETTING INTO THE CAB.

THE CRUSHER IS WORKED BY POWERFUL HYDRAULIC RAMS.

GARBAGE TRUCK

Smelly garbage trucks trundle around the streets collecting garbage from houses. The crew throw the garbage into the back of the truck. When the truck is full, it goes off to the local garbage dump to be emptied.

LIFTING TRASH CANS

Some containers are too heavy for the crew to lift. A machine grabs these containers, tips them up and shakes the garbage out into the truck.

DID YOU KNOW?

One garbage truck can collect all the garbage from a small town in a week. That's about 10,000 bags full!

TODAY, MANY GARBAGE TRUCKS RECYCLE SOME OF THE MATERIALS THEY COLLECT.

CARGO VAN

A van is like a small truck or a very big car! Vans can do hundreds of different jobs. Many trades people, such as builders and plumbers, have a van for moving their tools and materials.

CARGO SPACE

In the back of the van is a big space for cargo. The van has a sliding door at the side and a lift-up door at the back to make it easy to get the cargo in and out. A big van can carry two tons of cargo. That weighs the same as two cars.

DID YOU KNOW?

Some cargo vans are converted into camper vans. Inside there are beds, cupboards and a tiny kitchen.

PANELS AND WINDOWS

This type of van is called a panel van because it has metal panels instead of windows along the sides.

Some vans have windows instead. Some vans have a flat back with no body at all. Some are short, like this one, but others are much longer or taller.

THERE IS A POWERFUL ENGINE UNDER THE HOOD.

SOME VANS ARE CONVERTED INTO SMALL BUSES CALLED MINI-BUSES.

THE VAN HAS POWER- STEERING TO MAKE IT EASY TO DRIVE.

THERE ARE TWO PASSENGER SEATS NEXT TO THE DRIVER'S SEAT.

BACK DOORS

This van has a big lifting back door to make it easy to get big, heavy boxes in and out. Some big vans have a lift on the back.

ARMORED VANS ARE USED FOR CARRYING VALUABLES.

MAKING STEAM

Steam locomotives are moved along by the power of hot steam. The steam is made inside a big tank called a boiler. Water in the tank is heated by a fire to make the steam. The boiler works just like a kettle on a campsite fire.

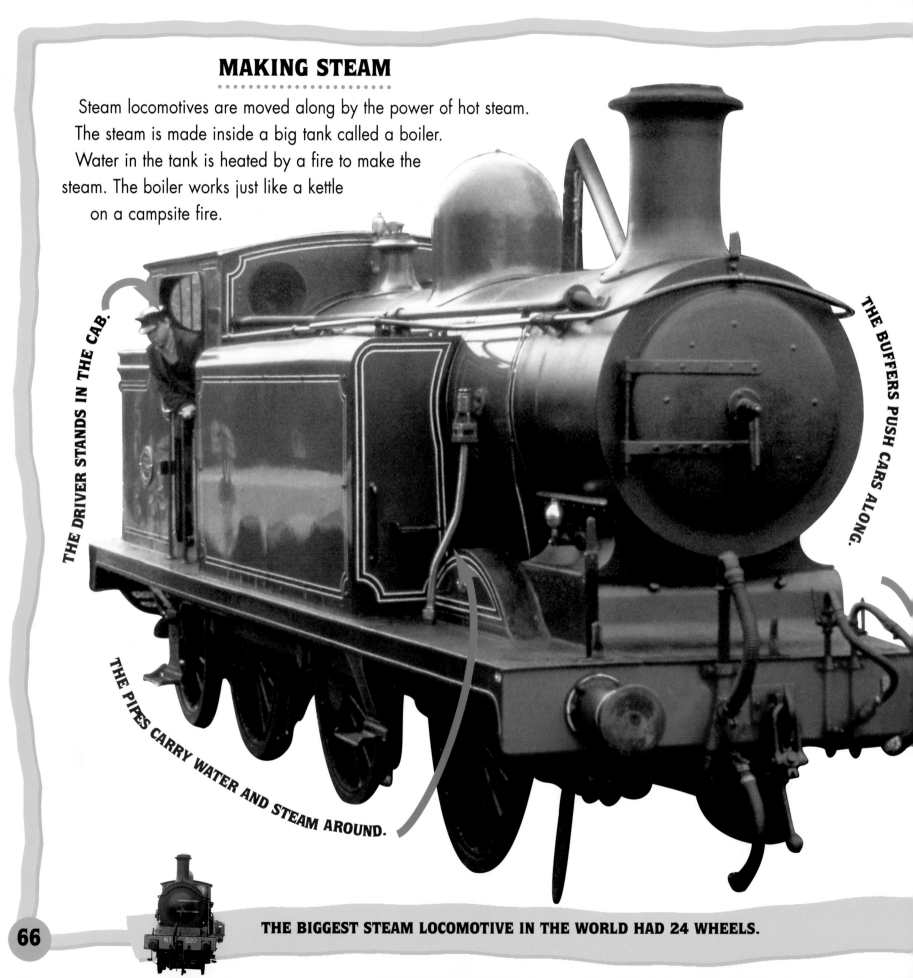

THE DRIVER STANDS IN THE CAB.

THE BUFFERS PUSH CARS ALONG.

THE PIPES CARRY WATER AND STEAM AROUND.

THE BIGGEST STEAM LOCOMOTIVE IN THE WORLD HAD 24 WHEELS.

STEAM TRAIN

A hundred years ago all trains were steam trains. They were pulled along by a puffing steam locomotive, leaving a cloud of smoke and steam behind.

PUSHING PISTONS

Steam from the boiler travels along pipes to cylinders which look like bicycle pumps. The steam pushes the pistons in the cylinders in and out. A rod joined to the piston makes the locomotive's wheels turn round.

FUNNEL FACTS

Steam and smoke come out of the funnel. Passengers in the carriages behind often get covered in bits of soot!

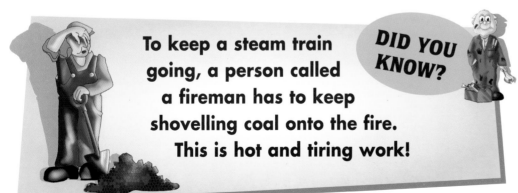

DID YOU KNOW?

To keep a steam train going, a person called a fireman has to keep shovelling coal onto the fire. This is hot and tiring work!

HIGH-SPEED TRAIN

Trains have come a long way since 1825 when the first passenger locomotive made its debut journey. Today, there are trains in Europe and the Far East capable of travelling at speeds greater than Formula 1 racing cars.

THE PANTOGRAPH COLLECTS ELECTRICITY FROM THE OVERHEAD CABLE.

THE SIDE VENTILATION PANELS KEEP THE POWER CAR COOL.

THE EUROSTAR TRAIN RUNNING BETWEEN ENGLAND AND FRANCE WAS LAUNCHED IN 1994.

CONTINENTAL CRUISERS

High-speed trains have been running in France since 1981.

Powerful engines, smooth tracks and air-cushion suspension all help these trains to travel at speeds of more than 185 mph.

DID YOU KNOW?

The Channel Tunnel is 31 miles long. It takes a Eurostar express twenty minutes to zoom through it.

THE NOSE IS STREAMLINED FOR HIGH SPEED.

CROSS-COUNTRY

Eurostar is an electric train that can travel at great speed. It is moved along by electric motors that make the wheels turn. The electricity for the motors comes from a cable above the track. It goes to one of the power cars at each end of the train and then to the motors.

SCIENCE FACT

This experimental Japanese train is powered by magnets. When launched, it will halve the journey time from Osaka to Tokyo.

THE DRIVER'S DOOR LEADS TO THE FRONT CAB.

IN 1990, A FRENCH TGV TRAIN REACHED A SPEED OF 320 MPH.

THE DRIVER SITS BEHIND THIS WINDOW.

THIS TRAIN GETS ELECTRICITY FROM A RAIL ON THE TRACK.

In big cities in Japan, workers are employed to get commuters onto the subway. This ensures that the trains are really packed!

DID YOU KNOW?

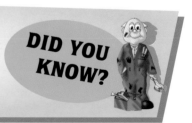

IN MANY BIG CITIES THE COMMUTER TRAINS TRAVEL UNDERGROUND.

COMMUTER TRAIN

Every morning millions of people jump onto commuter trains to travel to work in towns and cities. They all jump out when the trains arrive. At the end of the day they all jump back on again to travel home!

SPEEDING UP AND SLOWING DOWN

Commuter trains stop at several stations as they travel into cities. They must quickly whiz away from one station in order to get to the next stop as quickly as possible. Most commuter trains have powerful electric motors that make their wheels go round.

ALL ABOARD

Commuter trains are designed to carry as many people as possible. Inside the cars there are plenty of seats and lots of room for people to stand. There are wide doors so people can get on quickly when the train stops at a busy station.

DRIVER'S CAB

The driver controls the train's speed. He moves a lever to make the train speed up or slow down. If he accidentally lets go of the lever, the train automatically stops.

SOME COMMUTER TRAINS HAVE DOUBLE-DECKER CARS.

TROLLEY

If you live in a big city you might jump on a trolley instead of a bus. A trolley is a cross between a train and a bus. It travels on tracks like a train but goes through the busy streets like a bus.

MIXING WITH TRAFFIC

The tracks that a trolley travels on are called trolley lines. In the city center they go along the main streets. The trolleys get mixed up with the cars, buses and trucks. Trolleys are worked by electric motors, powered by cables above the street.

NO NOISE

Trolleys are quiet and clean. They often go through pedestrianised areas of the city where no cars or buses are allowed.

STANDING ROOM ONLY

Trolleys have three or four cars, like a short train. In the rush hour they are packed full of people. There are some seats inside, but also lots of space to stand. The trolleys stop at platforms in the street, where people jump on and off.

TROLLEYS OR STREETCARS IN SAN FRANCISCO ARE MOVED BY CABLES UNDER THE STREET.

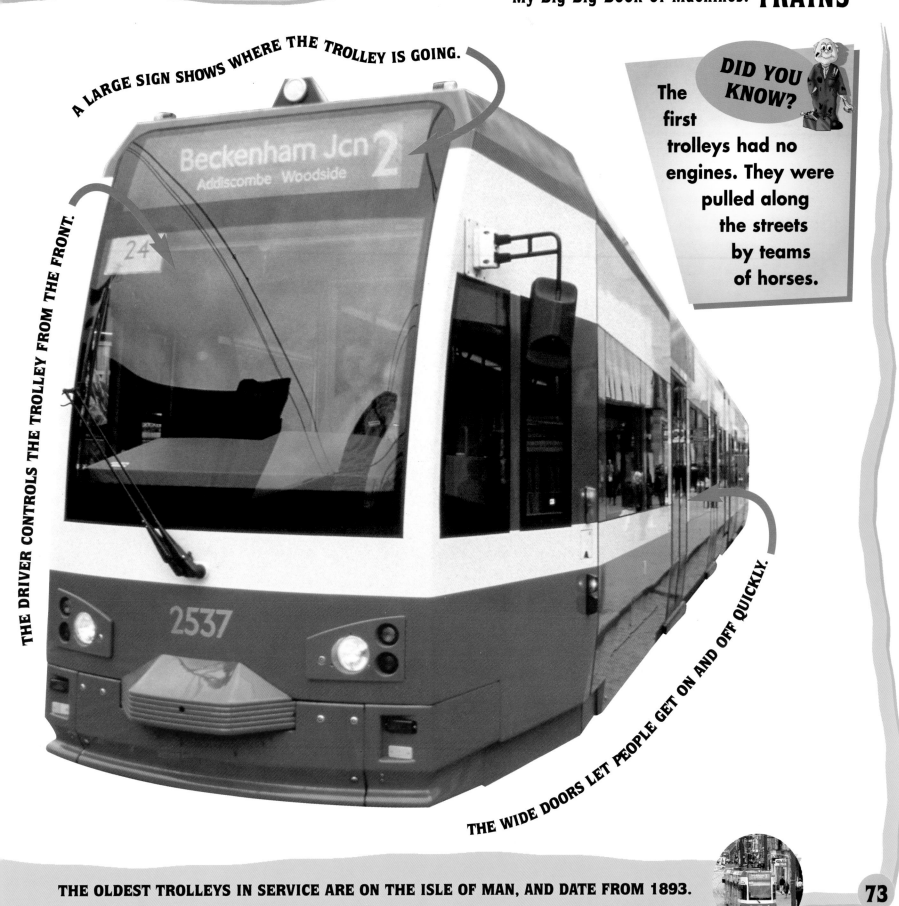

A LARGE SIGN SHOWS WHERE THE TROLLEY IS GOING.

Beckenham Jcn 2
Addiscombe Woodside

24

2537

THE DRIVER CONTROLS THE TROLLEY FROM THE FRONT.

DID YOU KNOW?

The first trolleys had no engines. They were pulled along the streets by teams of horses.

THE WIDE DOORS LET PEOPLE GET ON AND OFF QUICKLY.

THE OLDEST TROLLEYS IN SERVICE ARE ON THE ISLE OF MAN, AND DATE FROM 1893.

DID YOU KNOW?

The shunter's buffers have huge, strong springs inside. They stop the shunter from getting damaged when it bashes into wagons.

THE DRIVER'S CAB HAS WINDOWS ALL ROUND.

THESE METAL PANELS HAVE SLOTS TO LET THE ENGINE COOL DOWN.

A LADDER GOES UP TO THE CAB.

THESE RODS MAKE ALL THE WHEELS TURN TOGETHER.

IN THE U.S.A., MONSTER DIESEL LOCOMOTIVES ARE USED TO PULL FREIGHT TRAINS.

SHUNTING LOCOMOTIVE

Ashunter is a small, sturdy locomotive. You might see a shunter as you go through a busy station. It pushes and pulls carriages and wagons as it moves them onto the right part of the train track.

SORTING WAGONS

Shunters can push or pull. Pushing is also called shunting. When a shunter pushes, its buffers bump against the buffers of the car or wagon. The shunter also has a hook called a coupling at each end so that it can pull.

SHAKERS AND MOVERS

Shunters can be used for a variety of purposes. They can move passenger cars along train lines, as well as freight cars like the one shown above.

TRAIN COMING!

There are bright stripes painted on the front and back of the shunter. They help railroad workers see the shunter coming.

MONORAIL TRAIN

Not all trains travel on a track with two metal rails. A monorail train travels on a track with only one rail. They are a great way to get about in towns and cities. However, unfortunately there are only a few monorail tracks in the world.

MONORAIL MAGIC

Monorails are often found at theme parks and airport, like Heathrow. In Japan, some monorails are powered by magnets, and hover above the track rather than touching it.

CLEAN GETAWAY

This famous monorail runs through Sydney harbor in Australia, offering passengers striking views. It offers a quiet and easy way of getting around the city.

DID YOU KNOW?

A monorail train in Germany hangs underneath its track! The track is held up in the air on metal towers.

DESPITE THEIR FUTURISTIC IMAGE, MONORAILS HAVE BEEN AROUND FOR A CENTURY.

AUTOMATIC TRAINS

This monorail train has no driver. Everything works automatically. The train knows when to start and stop at stations, when to speed up and slow down, and when to open its doors. It is controlled by a computer.

THE WIDE DOORS LET PASSENGERS GET ON AND OFF WITH LOTS OF LUGGAGE.

THE LARGE FRONT WINDOW LETS PEOPLE SEE WHERE THE TRAIN IS GOING.

THE HINGE LETS THE TRAIN BEND AS IT GOES ROUND CORNERS.

BRITISH AIRWAYS

THE MOST FAMOUS MONORAILS ARE IN SYDNEY AND DISNEYWORLD, FLORIDA.

The smallest model railroad ever made was so tiny that the locomotive was only one centimetre long. Amazingly, it worked!

TINY PARTS

The miniature model steam locomotive is very small, but looks exactly like a real steam locomotive. Every pipe and lever works. There is even a tiny steam-powered whistle. Models like this take hundreds of hours to make.

THE PASSENGERS RIDE ON TINY WAGONS.

MODEL BUFFERS PROTECT THE TRAIN FROM BUMPS AT THE END OF THE TRACK.

CONCRETE BLOCKS SUPPORT THE TRACK.

MANY THEME PARKS LIKE ALTON TOWERS IN ENGLAND HAVE MINIATURE RAILROADS.

MINIATURE TRAIN

Miniature trains are much smaller than real steam trains, but they work in exactly the same way. They are often found in amusement parks, where they take children for rides.

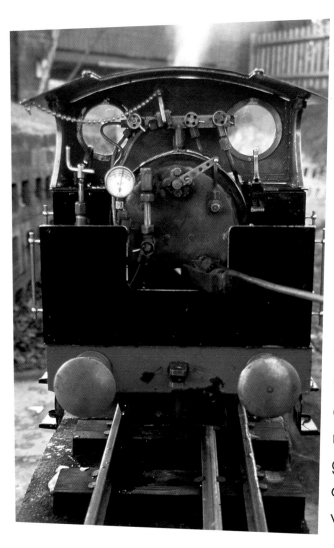

READY TO RUN

A miniature train needs a miniature track to travel on! Before it can start off, the driver lights a fire inside the locomotive to make the water inside boil. This makes the steam that pushes the train along. The driver must keep the fire going all the time, otherwise the train will grind to a halt.

DRIVING A MODEL

The model train driver dresses up like a real train driver. He sits behind the locomotive and uses miniature controls to make the train start and stop.

SOME PEOPLE HAVE OUTDOOR TRAIN SETS WITH STEAM TRAINS.

QUAD BIKE

The word 'quad' means four. A quad bike is a motorbike with four wheels! It is like a cross between a motorbike and a tractor. Riding a quad bike is easy because it can't fall over sideways!

4X4

The engine in a quad bike makes all the bike's wheels turn. it is like a 4x4 car.

STRONG MACHINES

Quad bikes have big motorbike engines to get up steep hills. They have strong springs on their wheels. The springs let the wheels move up and down on bumpy ground. Their chunky tires grip in even the deepest, stickiest mud.

THE METAL RACKS HOLD EQUIPMENT OR SUPPLIES.

THE LONGEST JUMP EVER MADE ON A QUAD BIKE WAS OVER 130 FEET.

FARMING BIKE

Farmers have quad bikes to get about on their farms. A quad bike can go over rough, muddy fields without any trouble. Farmers load food onto their quad bikes and zoom off across their fields to take the supplies to their sheep or cows.

Some people go racing on quad bikes. They race round grassy, slippery tracks in hilly fields.

DID YOU KNOW?

THE BIKES' CONTROLS ARE ON ITS HANDLEBARS.

THE DRIVER SITS ON A PADDED SEAT.

THESE MUD GUARDS STOP MUD FROM FLYING IN THE AIR.

QUAD BIKES ARE TWICE AS HEAVY AS ORDINARY MOTORBIKES.

81

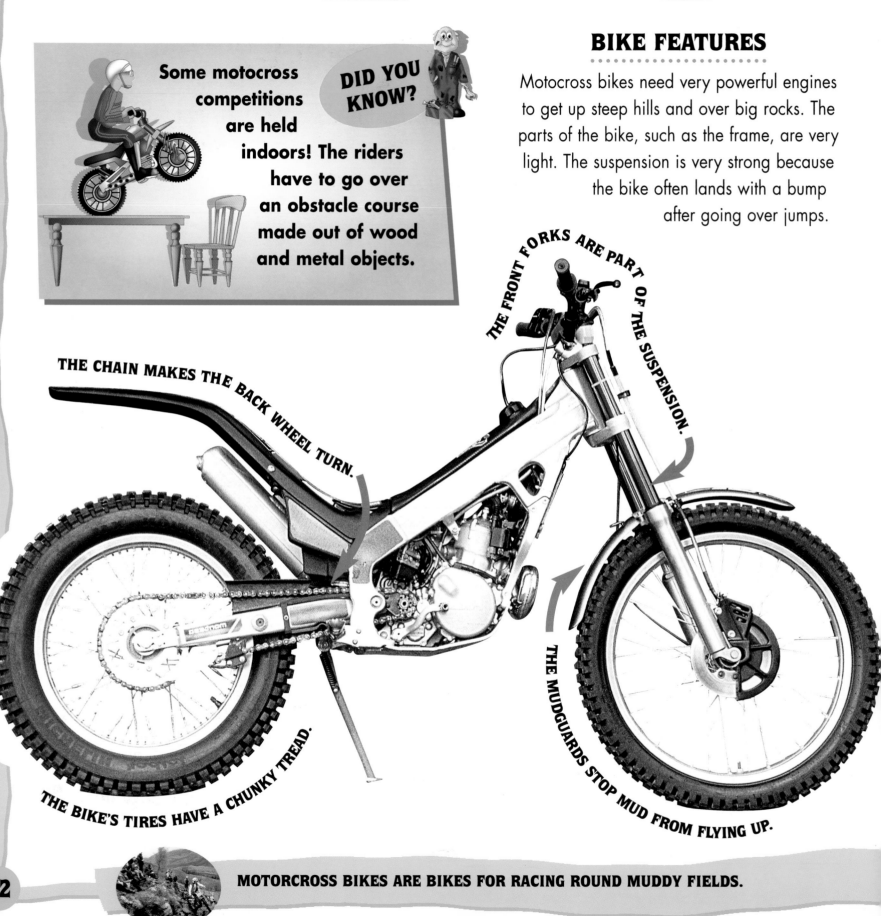

Some motocross competitions are held indoors! The riders have to go over an obstacle course made out of wood and metal objects.

DID YOU KNOW?

BIKE FEATURES

Motocross bikes need very powerful engines to get up steep hills and over big rocks. The parts of the bike, such as the frame, are very light. The suspension is very strong because the bike often lands with a bump after going over jumps.

THE FRONT FORKS ARE PART OF THE SUSPENSION.

THE CHAIN MAKES THE BACK WHEEL TURN.

THE BIKE'S TIRES HAVE A CHUNKY TREAD.

THE MUDGUARDS STOP MUD FROM FLYING UP.

MOTORCROSS BIKES ARE BIKES FOR RACING ROUND MUDDY FIELDS.

MOTOCROSS BIKES

A motocross bike is a motorbike designed for going through gooey mud and deep streams, bumping over rocks and logs, and up and down very steep hills. The souped-up suspension means that the bike can take a lot of punishment.

MOTOCROSS RIDING

A motorbike trial is a test designed for motocross riders. The riders must ride round a steep, rocky, muddy course, trying not to fall off or even touch the ground with their feet. They need lots of skill to control their bikes and stay balanced.

NO FRILLS BIKE

Motocross bikes don't have any parts that they don't need, like headlights or blinkers. Leaving these items out helps keep the weight of the bike down.

MOTOCROSS BIKES ARE USED IN RALLIES ACROSS DESERTS.

SCOOTER

Scooters are motorbikes slimmed down for an urban environment. They work on the same principle, but have less powerful engines and are much lighter than proper bikes. The controls for breaking and accelerating are on the handlebars.

CLASSIC SCOOTER

This is what most scooters looked like before the 1990s. They had a big, flat seat and a gap between the engine and the handlebars for the rider's legs.

SCOOTER HISTORY

A scooter does not have a frame like a larger motorbike. It has a small engine under the seat, just in front of the back wheel. Its wheels are smaller than the wheels on a normal motorbike, too. Scooters are very popular because they are easy to ride and cheap to run.

CHILDREN CAN BUY TOY SCOOTERS WITH SMALL ENGINES.

SCOOTER PARTS

The scooter was invented in Italy in the 1950s. Scooters soon became popular with teenagers for riding around with their friends. Scooters didn't change much until the 1990s. Then they began to look a bit more modern, like the one here.

DID YOU KNOW?

In the 1960s and 1970s, people called mods rode scooters in large gangs. They decorated their scooters with dozens of wing mirrors.

CONTROLS FOR SPEEDING UP AND SLOWING DOWN ARE ON THE HANDLEBARS.

A PASSENGER HANGS ONTO THIS HANDLE.

GILERA

Runner

THE FAT EXHAUST MAKES THE SCOOTER QUIET.

THE FUEL TANK IS UNDER THE SEAT.

SCOOTERS ALSO COME IN FOLD-UP FORMS THAT CAN BE CARRIED AROUND TOWN.

People who ride custom bikes often wear customised clothes as well! These are made from black leather, and have metal studs all over them.

DID YOU KNOW?

CUSTOM BIKES HAVE LONG FRONT FORKS.

THE SEAT IS LOWER THAN ON OTHER BIKES.

THE OWNER KEEPS ALL THE METAL VERY SHINY.

THE BODY IS CAREFULLY PAINTED.

CHOPPED–UP BIKES

A chopper is a type of custom bike. It gets its name because owners of choppers have chopped off parts of the bike to make them lighter. Choppers have very low seats. Riding one is like sitting back in an armchair!

THREE-WHEELED CUSTOM BIKES HAVE TWO SEATS SIDE-BY-SIDE.

CUSTOM BIKE

A custom bike is a motorbike with parts cut off and other parts put on! Bike owners customise their bikes to make them look different to other bikes. They often display them at shows.

DRAG RACING

A drag race is a sprint race between two monster customised bikes. The bikes have two or three engines and a huge back wheel to grip the track. The riders lie on top and hold tight as their bikes screech along in a cloud of smoke!

CUSTOM FIRSTS

The first custom bikes were made in the U.S.A. from Harley Davidson motorcycles. Their owners cut off parts to make them faster.

SOME PEOPLE HAVE CUSTOMISED SCOOTERS AS WELL AS MOTORBIKES!

RACING BIKE

Riders race furiously against each other on their powerful racing bikes. The bikes are designed to speed up and slow down quickly, and to fly along the straights at more than 155 mph.

MIND YOUR KNEES

Racing riders often lean over so far that their knees nearly touch the track! Strong pads are worn for protection.

PREPARING TO RACE

Most races are held on special race tracks. To make the races fair, all the bikes must have the same size of engine, and they must be the same weight. A team of mechanics spend hours before the race making sure the bike will go as fast as possible.

TAKING A CORNER

You have to be very brave and skillful to ride a racing bike. Going round the corners fast is very tricky. The riders lean right over as they turn. This stops the bike from flipping over sideways. They wear thick leather clothes to protect them if they fall off.

BECAUSE THEY ARE SO LIGHT, RACING BIKES CAN REACH MUCH GREATER SPEEDS THAN CARS.

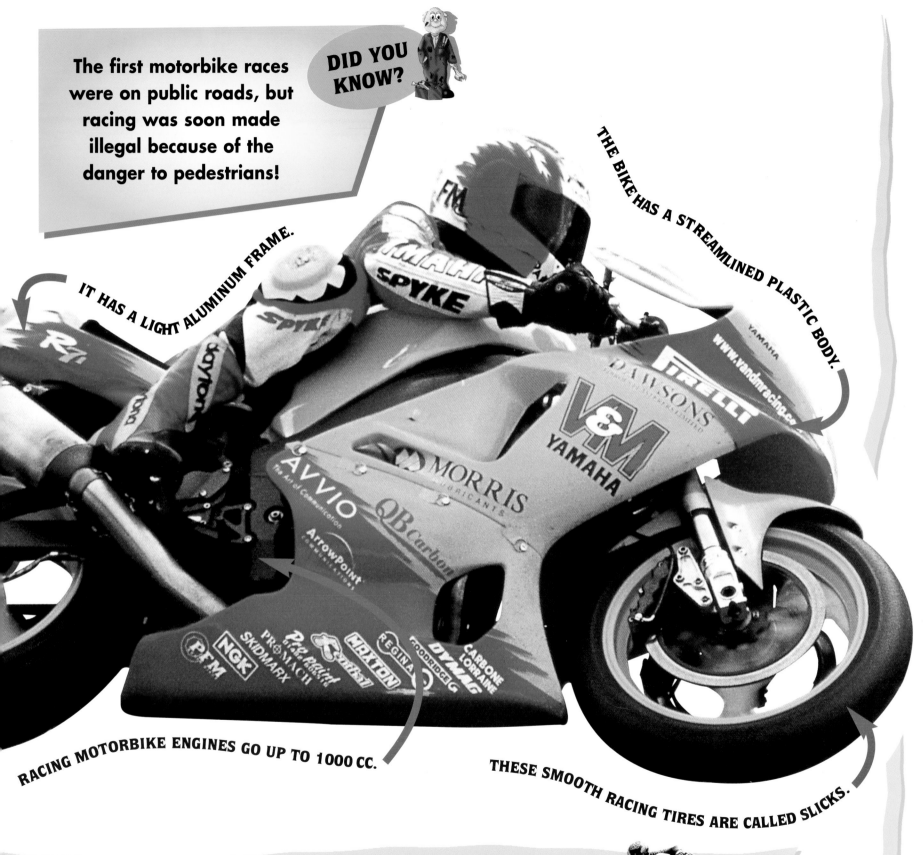

DID YOU KNOW?

The first motorbike races were on public roads, but racing was soon made illegal because of the danger to pedestrians!

THE BIKE HAS A STREAMLINED PLASTIC BODY.

IT HAS A LIGHT ALUMINUM FRAME.

RACING MOTORBIKE ENGINES GO UP TO 1000 CC.

THESE SMOOTH RACING TIRES ARE CALLED SLICKS.

SPEEDWAY RIDERS RACE AROUND OVAL DIRT TRACKS.

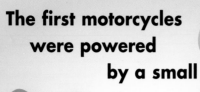

The first motorcycles were powered by a small steam engine under the seat. Riding one was quite dangerous!

DID YOU KNOW?

MOTORBIKE COLLECTORS

There aren't many vintage bikes left. The ones that are left are very valuable. Their owners look after them carefully. They keep them clean and shiny, and take them to motorbike shows. They also ride them in vintage motorcycle rallies.

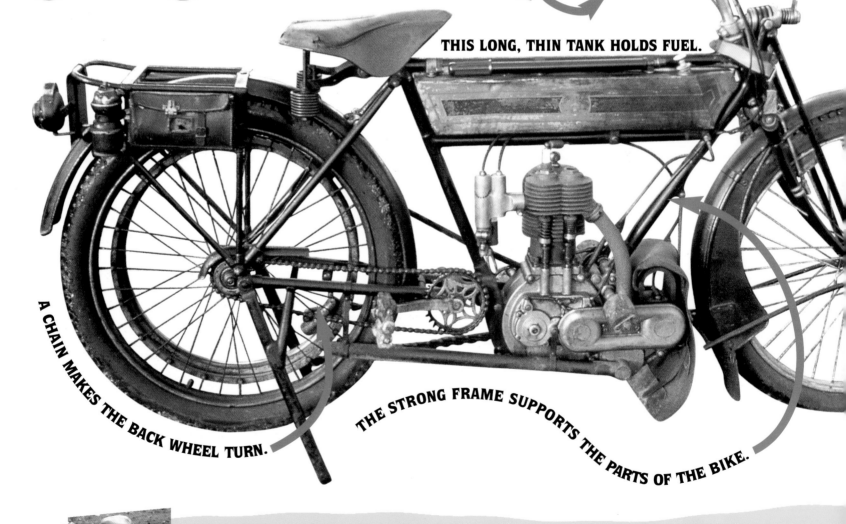

THE HANDLEBARS ARE LIKE THOSE ON A BICYCLE.

THIS LONG, THIN TANK HOLDS FUEL.

A CHAIN MAKES THE BACK WHEEL TURN.

THE STRONG FRAME SUPPORTS THE PARTS OF THE BIKE.

THE FIRST MOTORBIKE PASSENGERS WERE PULLED ALONG IN CARTS!

VINTAGE MOTORBIKE

A vintage motorbike is a really, really old motorbike. Vintage motorbikes look like bicycles with engines added to them. They can be over one hundred years old.

VINTAGE PARTS

Vintage motorbikes have a monster leather seat that looks like a big bicycle seat. There are big springs underneath for comfort. Behind the seat is a luggage rack. The riders would have worn leather clothes, and big leather gloves, but no crash helmet.

SINGLE CYLINDER

This bike has a small engine with just one cylinder and piston. It also has pedals in case the engine breaks down!

THE FIRST MOTORBIKES HAD NO BRAKES!

SUPERBIKE

Superbikes are the kings of the motorbike world. They are big, expensive and super fast. They are also very exciting to ride. Every bike rider would like to own a superbike!

SMOOTH SHAPES

The front of a superbike is smooth and curved. This helps the bike speed quickly through the air.

FAST AND FURIOUS

Superbikes are often racing bikes that are allowed to go on the road. They can reach a speed of 60 mph in less than three seconds. That would leave any sports car a long way behind. They can also scream to speeds of more than 155 mph.

THE FIRST SUPERBIKE WAS THE HONDA CB750, BUILT IN 1968.

MONSTER ENGINE

Underneath the superbike's seat is a huge engine. It is as big as the engine in a family car, and just as powerful. It makes a noisy roar as the bike whizzes off down the road. Gas for the engine is stored in the tank by the seat.

Superbikes are so powerful that the front wheel lifts of the ground as they start off. This is called doing a wheelie.

DID YOU KNOW?

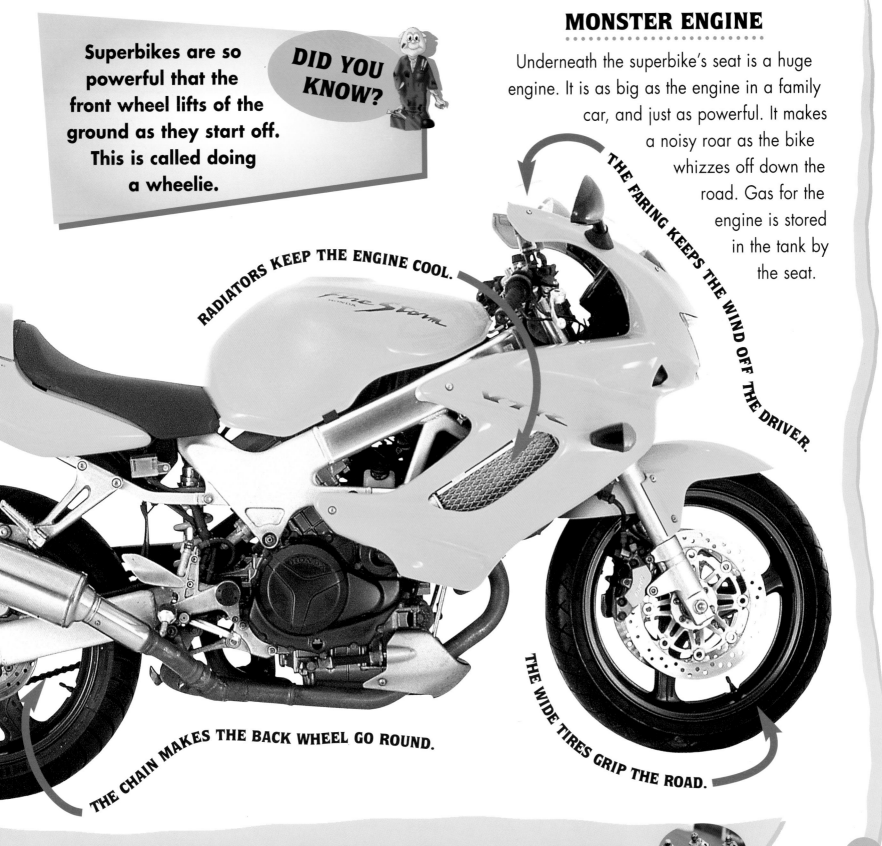

THE FARING KEEPS THE WIND OFF THE DRIVER.

RADIATORS KEEP THE ENGINE COOL.

THE CHAIN MAKES THE BACK WHEEL GO ROUND.

THE WIDE TIRES GRIP THE ROAD.

Patrol car drivers take special driving lessons before they are allowed to chase criminals in their cars.

DID YOU KNOW?

RADIO CALLS

The police officers in a patrol car talk to the police station by radio. Over the radio they can ask for help from officers in other cars, or request an ambulance. The radio operator at the police station can also give the officers directions or other instructions.

THE FLASHING LIGHTS ARE BOLTED TO THE ROOF.

THE CAR BEARS THE BADGE OF THE POLICE ORGANISATION.

POLICE FORCES ALSO USE VANS FOR MOVING LOTS OF OFFICERS ABOUT.

POLICE PATROL CAR

Police officers patrol town and city streets in their patrol cars. If there is a crime or an accident, they rush to the scene in their powerful vehicles to try to sort the problem out.

THE WINDOW BARS STOP PRISONERS ESCAPING.

736

LIGHTS AND SIRENS

A patrol car has sirens that make a loud wailing noise, and bright blue flashing lights. When the police officers are in a hurry, they turn on the sirens and lights so that other drivers and pedestrians can hear and see them coming, and move out of the way.

MARKED CARS

Police patrol cars are painted with bright red or orange stripes so that people can see them easily. They have 'POLICE' written on them.

W827 AKP

POLICE PATROL CARS HAVE POWERFUL ENGINES SO THAT THEY CAN KEEP UP DURING PURSUITS.

FIRE ENGINE

When fire fighters get an emergency call at their fire station they jump into their fire engines and race to the scene. The fire engine helps the fire fighters to put out fires and rescue people from burning buildings.

FIRE-FIGHTING EQUIPMENT

A fire engine carries lots of fire-fighting equipment. There are ladders for climbing up to windows and onto roofs, and there is breathing equipment that enables fire fighters to enter smoky buildings. There is also cutting equipment used to free people trapped in cars after road accidents.

SPRAYING WATER

When the fire engine reaches the fire, the fire fighters unroll long pipes called hoses. They aim them at the fire. They turn on the engine's powerful pump, which pushes water along the hoses and into the flames.

OLD FIRE ENGINES WERE PULLED BY HORSES. THEIR PUMPS WERE WORKED BY HAND.

HOSE IN THE AIR

This fire engine has a platform that rises into the air. A fire fighter stands on the platform and sprays water through a building's windows.

Fire fighters need to be very strong. When the water comes out of a hose, the force can knock a fire fighter over backwards.

DID YOU KNOW?

FLASHING LIGHTS AND SIRENS WARN PEOPLE THAT THE FIRE ENGINE IS COMING.

THE CREW TRAVEL IN THIS CAB.

INSIDE THERE IS A HUGE TANK FULL OF WATER.

DENNIS

M889 OKE

AIRPORTS HAVE THEIR OWN FIRE ENGINES THAT SPRAY FOAM ON FIRE.

97

DID YOU KNOW? When the ambulance is rushing to hospital, one paramedic drives the ambulance and the other looks after the patients.

CALLING AN AMBULANCE

Every ambulance has a radio so that the paramedics can talk to their control center and the hospital. The control center tells the paramedics where there are accidents or emergencies. The paramedics tell the hospital what is wrong with the patients and when they are going to arrive.

BRIGHT STRIPES MAKE THE AMBULANCE EASY TO SEE.

FLASHING LIGHTS WARN DRIVERS THAT THE AMBULANCE IS COMING.

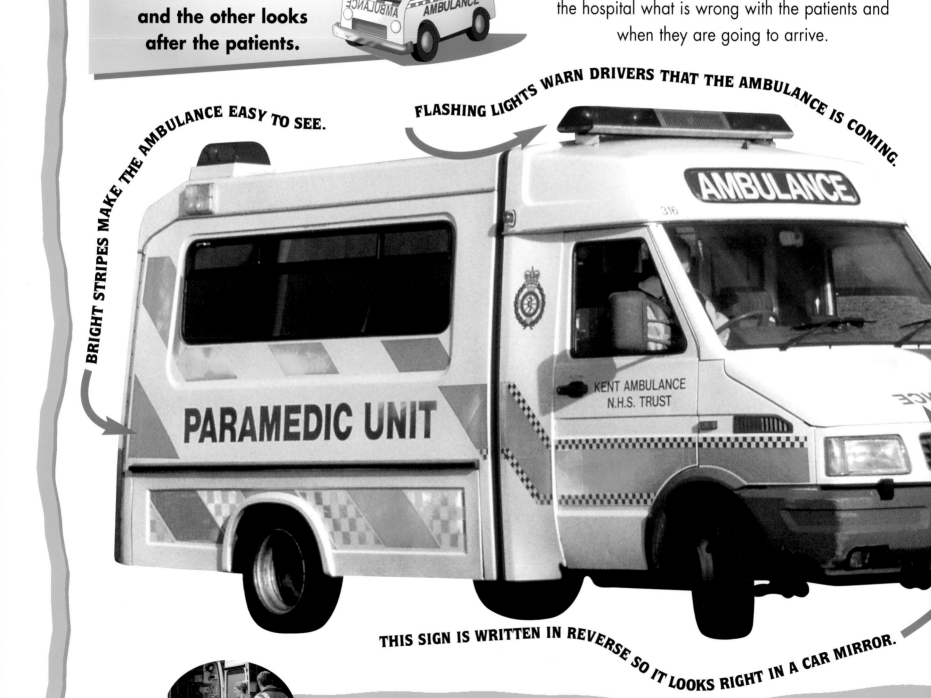

PARAMEDIC UNIT

AMBULANCE

KENT AMBULANCE N.H.S. TRUST

316

THIS SIGN IS WRITTEN IN REVERSE SO IT LOOKS RIGHT IN A CAR MIRROR.

THE LARGEST AMBULANCES ARE 59 FEET LONG ALLIGATOR JUMBULANCES.

AMBULANCE

An ambulance is an emergency vehicle that rushes people to hospital. The people might be very ill or they may have been in an accident. A person called a paramedic looks after the people inside the ambulance.

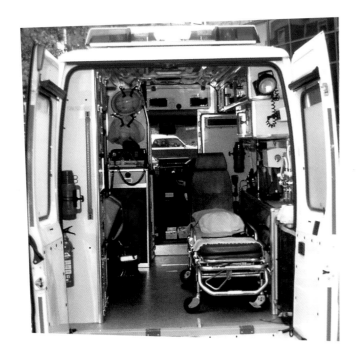

AMBULANCE EQUIPMENT

The back of an ambulance is crammed full of useful equipment. On each side there are beds called stretchers. The paramedics take them out to carry patients into the ambulance. There is also first-aid equipment, such as bandages and splints for broken bones.

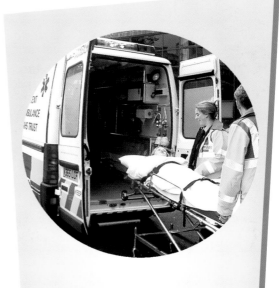

EASY ACCESS

Ambulances have wide doors at the rear so patients can be placed in the van carefully and easily.

AN AIR AMBULANCE IS A HELICOPTER THAT GETS PEOPLE TO HOSPITAL IN DOUBLE-QUICK TIME.

LIFEBOAT

A lifeboat is a fast, tough boat that rescues people from the sea. A lifeboat can go to sea in very rough weather. It bashes through the big waves with its strong hull.

LAUNCHING A LIFEBOAT

When an emergency call comes the lifeboat crew have to be ready to launch their boat into the sea as quickly as possible. In this picture, the crew are already dressed in their waterproof suits and life jackets.

LIFEBOAT RADIOS

This lifeboat has tall radio aerials on its deck. They let the crew talk to the coast guard and rescue helicopters using a radio.

BEFORE ENGINES WERE INVENTED, LIFEBOAT CREWS USED TO ROW OUT TO RESCUE PEOPLE.

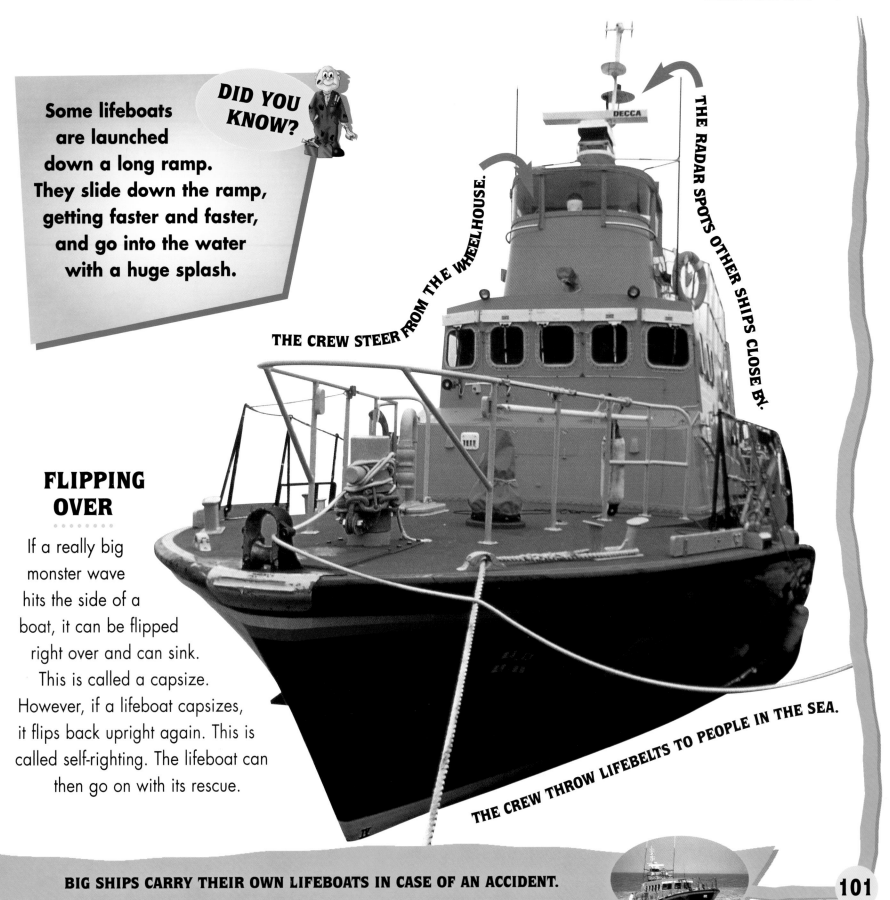

Some lifeboats are launched down a long ramp. They slide down the ramp, getting faster and faster, and go into the water with a huge splash.

DID YOU KNOW?

THE CREW STEER FROM THE WHEELHOUSE.

THE RADAR SPOTS OTHER SHIPS CLOSE BY.

FLIPPING OVER

If a really big monster wave hits the side of a boat, it can be flipped right over and can sink. This is called a capsize. However, if a lifeboat capsizes, it flips back upright again. This is called self-righting. The lifeboat can then go on with its rescue.

THE CREW THROW LIFEBELTS TO PEOPLE IN THE SEA.

BIG SHIPS CARRY THEIR OWN LIFEBOATS IN CASE OF AN ACCIDENT.

DID YOU KNOW?

The most famous police patrol bikes are Harley Davidsons. They are used by officers of the California Highway Patrol in the U.S.A.

A HIGH WINDSHIELD KEEPS WIND AND RAIN OFF THE RIDER.

STRONG BRAKES MAKE THE BIKE STOP QUICKLY.

THIS STAND STOPS THE BIKE FALLING OVER WHEN IT IS STATIONARY.

POLICE

KENT COUNTY CONSTABULARY

TA 45

HONDA

POLICE BIKES ARE OFTEN USED TO ESCORT VIP'S AROUND BUSY CITIES.

POLICE PATROL BIKE

Police officers zip up and down motorways and through busy city streets on their patrol bikes. The bikes are large and heavy, with big engines. The officers can quickly reach the scene of an accident on these mighty machines.

PATROL BIKE JOBS

Police officers often drive along busy roads watching out for people driving badly. They also ride ahead and behind extra large vehicles on the road to warn other drivers about the vehicles. The officers wear helmets and bright yellow jackets.

BIKE EQUIPMENT

A police bike carries lots of useful equipment. It has a radio that the police officer uses to talk to other officers. Boxes on the back of the bike are called panniers. Inside there are useful items such as speed-checking equipment.

LIGHTS AND SIRENS

A patrol bike has flashing lights on the front and back to warn people that the bike is coming. It also has loud sirens.

POLICE BIKES NEED TO BE VERY FAST TO KEEP UP WITH CRIMINALS.

LADDER TRUCK

ire fighters take a ladder truck when they are called to fight a fire in a tall building. The truck has a very long ladder that reaches high into the air. This allows fire fighters to rescue people in high places as well as putting out blazes in tall buildings.

LIGHTS AND SIRENS

On the front of the truck there are flashing lights and horribly loud sirens. There are also floodlights on the ladder's platform.

CLIMBING HIGH

On the end of the ladder there is a platform with a water nozzle. A fire fighter stands on the platform and sprays water down onto a fire or through a window. The water reaches the nozzle through a hose that goes right up the ladder.

THE EQUIPMENT IS STORED IN THESE LOCKERS.

SMALL LADDER TRUCKS ARE USED FOR SERVICING STREET LIGHTS.

TELESCOPIC LADDER

This ladder is a telescopic ladder. It is made up of four sections. Each section slides inside the one below. The sections slide out to make the ladder longer. The ladder sits on top of a turntable on the back of the truck.

DID YOU KNOW?

The ladder on a large ladder truck can reach as high as the 11th storey of a skyscraper.

A POWERFUL PUMP SENDS WATER TO THE LADDER'S WATER NOZZLE.

THE CREW TRAVEL IN THIS CAB.

THESE METAL FEET COME OUT TO STOP THE TRUCK TOPPLING OVER.

LADDER CO. 8

ST. PAUL FIRE

A LADDER TRUCK IS ALSO CALLED A TURNTABLE LADDER.

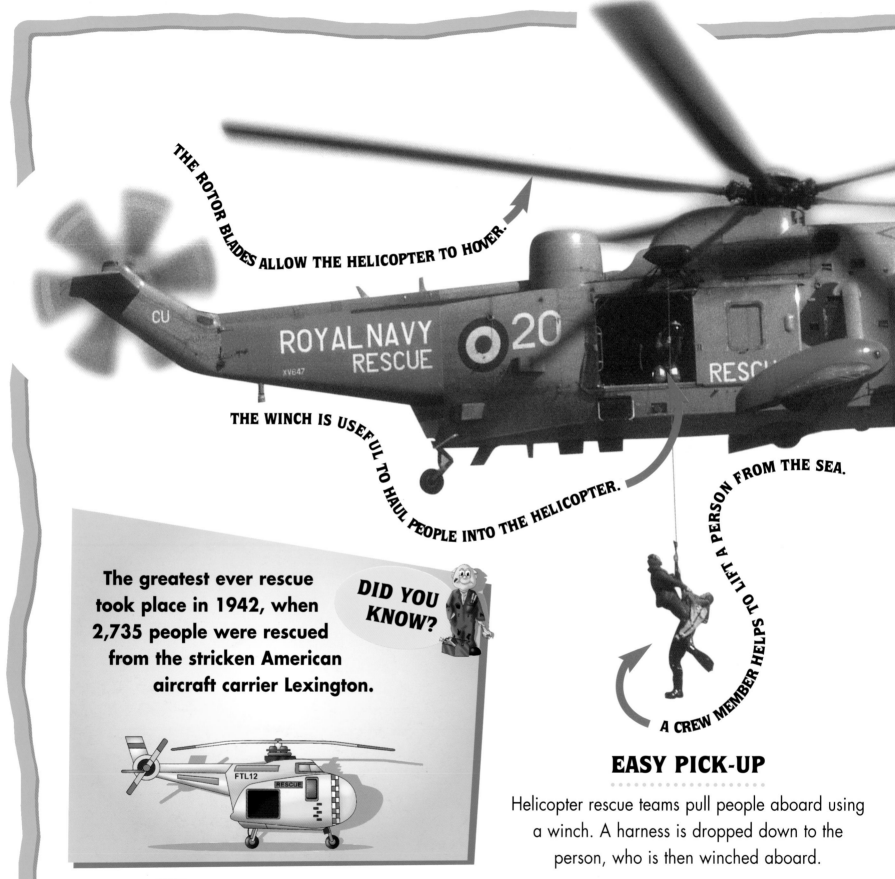

THE ROTOR BLADES ALLOW THE HELICOPTER TO HOVER.

ROYAL NAVY RESCUE

CU

XV647

20

RESCU

THE WINCH IS USEFUL TO HAUL PEOPLE INTO THE HELICOPTER.

A CREW MEMBER HELPS TO LIFT A PERSON FROM THE SEA.

The greatest ever rescue took place in 1942, when 2,735 people were rescued from the stricken American aircraft carrier Lexington.

DID YOU KNOW?

FTL12

RESCUE

EASY PICK-UP

Helicopter rescue teams pull people aboard using a winch. A harness is dropped down to the person, who is then winched aboard.

HELICOPTERS ARE ABLE TO HOVER FOR LONG PERIODS OF TIME.

AIR-SEA RESCUE

People often get into trouble at sea. Sometimes their boats sink. Sometimes they are washed out to sea from the shore. An air-sea rescue helicopter flies out to sea and picks them up without landing.

PLUCKED FROM THE SEA

Helicopters and lifeboats often work together rescuing people adrift at sea. The lifeboat will often pick up people from the water, who are then winched aboard a helicopter and whisked off to the nearest hospital.

MOUNTAIN RESCUE

Air-sea rescue helicopters also work in mountains. They rescue walkers and climbers who have had accidents. They often have to fly to places where normal planes could not go. Sometimes they hover very close to steep cliffs.

THE OLDEST LIFESAVING ORGANISATION IN THE WORLD IS THE 175 YEAR OLD BRITISH R.N.L.I.

107

FRONT-END LOADER

If you've got a monster pile of rubble to move, you need a loader like this. You see front-end loaders working on building sites, pushing soil and rubble about, picking it up and dumping it onto trucks that carry it away.

RUBBLE MOVING

The front-end loader picks up rubble with its huge front bucket. The driver aims at the pile of rubble and lowers the bucket to the ground. He drives into the rubble so the bucket fills up. Then he lifts the bucket up and drives away.

FOLDING ARM

This loader has a digging arm called a backhoe. The arm folds up to stop it swinging about as the loader moves along.

OIL POWER

Powerful rams make the loader's arms move up and down and make the bucket tip. The pistons look like bicycle pumps. Oil is pumped into the ram to make the pistons move in or out. The driver works the rams with levers in the cab.

LOADERS ARE STRONG ENOUGH TO LIFT THEMSELVES OFF THE GROUND WITH THEIR ARMS.

DID YOU KNOW? The driver's seat swings round so that he can work the loader at the front or the digging arm at the back.

THESE THICK PIPES CARRY OIL TO THE RAMS.

THE BIG WINDOWS GIVE THE DRIVER A GOOD VIEW.

THE BUCKET HAS STRONG TEETH.

THE CHUNKY TIRES GRIP IN MUDDY GROUND.

THESE FEET COME DOWN TO STOP THE LOADER TIPPING OVER.

A LOADER COULD EASILY LIFT A SMALL CAR IN ITS BUCKET.

CHANGING BUCKETS

The driver can change the wide bucket for a narrow bucket or another tool, such as a road drill or a lifting hook.

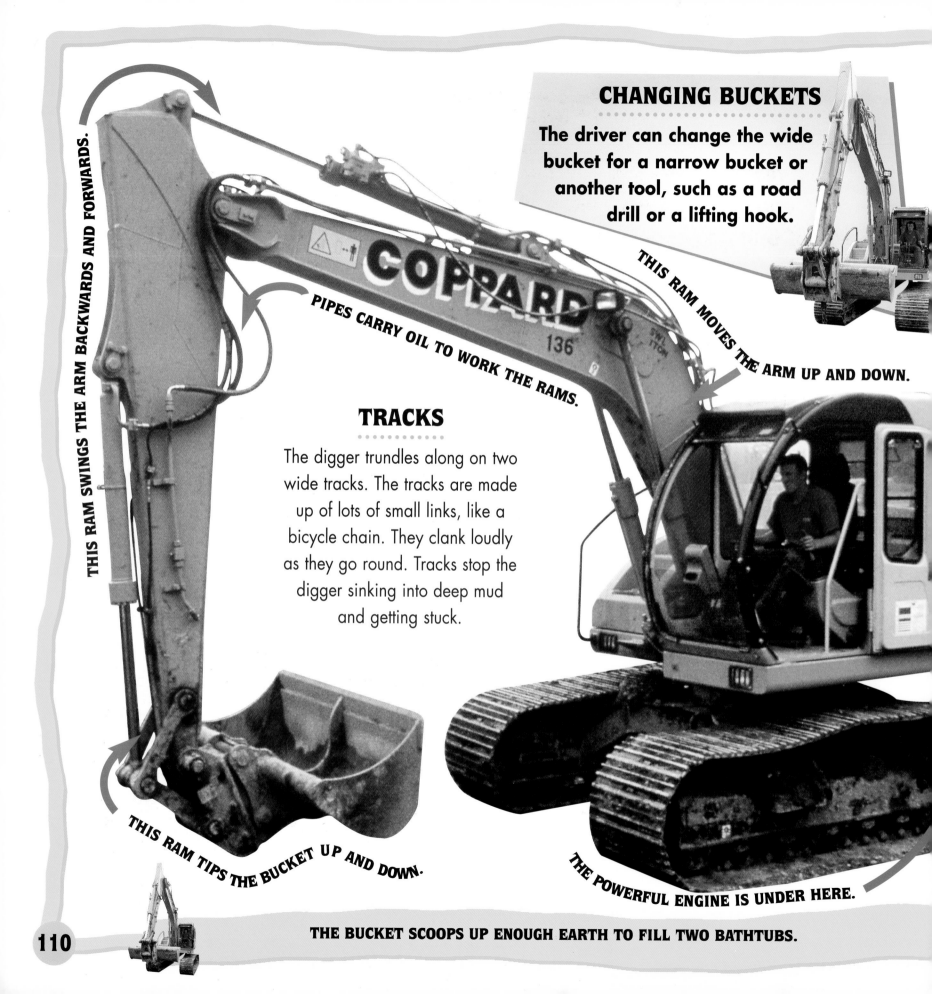

THIS RAM SWINGS THE ARM BACKWARDS AND FORWARDS.

PIPES CARRY OIL TO WORK THE RAMS.

THIS RAM MOVES THE ARM UP AND DOWN.

COPPARD

136

TRACKS

The digger trundles along on two wide tracks. The tracks are made up of lots of small links, like a bicycle chain. They clank loudly as they go round. Tracks stop the digger sinking into deep mud and getting stuck.

THIS RAM TIPS THE BUCKET UP AND DOWN.

THE POWERFUL ENGINE IS UNDER HERE.

THE BUCKET SCOOPS UP ENOUGH EARTH TO FILL TWO BATHTUBS.

DIGGER

In a few minutes this mechanical digger could dig a hole big enough to bury itself in! Diggers dig holes for underground parts of buildings, and trenches for underground pipes and cables.

MECHANICAL ARM

A digger's arm is like a person's arm, but it has rams instead of muscles to make it bend. The arm reaches down into the ground and scoops up out soil with its enormous bucket. The driver uses pedals and levers to work the arm and move the digger about.

DID YOU KNOW? There are mini diggers as well as big diggers. Mini diggers are smaller than cars. They often dig holes inside houses!

MOBILE CRANE

Have you ever seen a vehicle like this rumbling past? This truck with a crane on its back is called a mobile crane. Mobile cranes work on building sites. They lift heavy pieces of buildings into place.

SETTING UP

The driver must set up the crane before it can do any lifting. He parks the crane and puts down metal feet that stop it tipping over sideways. Then he lifts the boom. It can extend until it is five times as long as the truck.

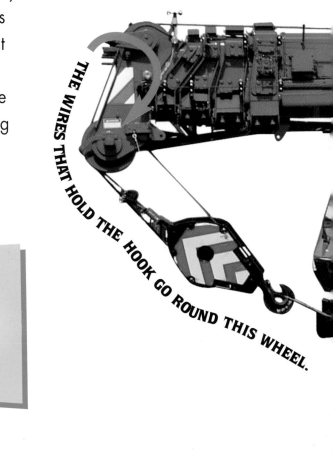

THE WIRES THAT HOLD THE HOOK GO ROUND THIS WHEEL.

DID YOU KNOW? There are floating mobile cranes, too. They work at sea, lifting wrecks from the sea bed.

A BIG MOBILE CRANE CAN REACH MORE THAN 260 FEET INTO THE AIR.

BOOMS AND HOOKS

This crane has a long arm called a boom that reaches high into the air. A massive hook hangs from the end of the boom. It lifts objects up and down. The hook swings about on strong metal wires.

CRANE CONTROLS

The driver works the crane from a small cab at the bottom of the boom. He pulls and pushes levers and presses on pedals.

THE BOTTOM OF THE BOOM SWIVELS FROM SIDE TO SIDE.

THIS IS THE CAB WHERE THE DRIVER SITS.

A MOBILE CRANE IS SO STRONG THAT IT COULD LIFT 30 FAMILY CARS AT ONCE.

The first farmers did not have tractors, or even horses. They pulled their ploughs themselves.

PLOUGHING A FIELD

The farmer attaches the plough to the back of a tractor. The tractor pulls the plough backwards and forwards across the field, like a person mowing a lawn. It then lifts the plough out of the soil as it turns round at the end of the field.

A STRONG FRAME SUPPORTS THE BLADES.

THIS MECHANISM LIFTS THE PLOUGH UP AND DOWN.

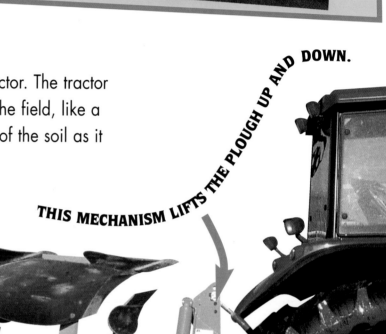

THE BLADES HAVE VERY SHARP POINTS.

THIS WHEEL STOPS THE BLADES DIGGING TOO FAR INTO THE SOIL.

 **IN MANY COUNTRIES PLOUGHS ARE PULLED BY HORSE, OX OR BUFFALO.**

PLOUGH

If you see birds flocking around a tractor in a field, the farmer might be ploughing. A plough digs over the soil to make it ready for new crops to be grown. The birds are looking for worms that the plough digs up.

MAKING FURROWS

The plough has 10 curved metal blades. Each blade slices into the soil. As the soil slides along the blade, it is lifted up and flipped over. This brings fresh soil to the surface. The lines of earth left behind the plough are called furrows.

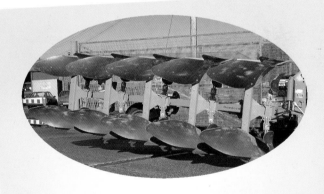

FIVE FURROWS

This plough has five blades on each side. It makes five furrows next to each other at the same time.

THE PLOUGH WAS INVENTED MORE THAN 9,000 YEARS AGO.

COMBINE HARVESTER

Combine harvesters are machines that combine reaping (cutting corn) with threshing (separating the grain). They save farmers a great deal of time when it comes to harvesting the crops.

HARVEST TIME

This part of the combine harvester is called the reel. It sweeps the stalks of the crop into the cutting bar, separating the grain, which then begins a journey up an elevator into the grain tank.

JACK OF ALL TRADES

Some combine harvesters can bale hay, too. The stalks are separated from the grain and sent to a different compartment, where they are packed into bales.

ENORMOUS ENGINE

Some of the most powerful high-tech combine harvesters have 500 brake horsepower engines. These are bigger than those found in nearly all sports cars.

MODERN HARVESTERS HAVE ON-BOARD COMPUTERS TO HELP THE FARMER.

THE FARMER SITS IN THIS CABIN.

THE CUTTING BAR CUTS THE CROPS.

DID YOU KNOW?

The first combine harvester was invented in 1835, and had to be pulled by horses!

NEW HOLLAND

FX38

NEW HOLLAND

THE REEL SWEEPS THE STALKS INTO THE MACHINE.

EARLY HARVESTERS DID NOT HAVE CABINS, SO THE FARMER ENDED UP COVERED IN CORN!

THE CAB KEEPS THE FARMER WARM AND DRY.

THE FARMER USES THESE FLOOD LAMPS TO WORK AT NIGHT.

NEW HOLLAND TM150

THE BIG WHEELS LET THE TRACTOR GO OVER BUMPY GROUND.

THE FIRST TRACTORS WERE STEAM POWERED. THEY WERE CALLED TRACTION ENGINES.

TRACTOR

Farming would be very hard work without a tractor! A tractor does many different jobs. It drives easily across steep, muddy fields, and pulls other farm machines such as ploughs and trailers.

ENGINE AND WHEELS

The tractor has a big, powerful diesel engine in front of the cab. It moves the tractor along and is also used to work other farm machinery. The tractor's huge wheels stop it sinking into the mud, while its chunky tires stop it slipping about.

WORKING MACHINERY

At the back of the tractor is a hook for towing a trailer, and an arm for lifting ploughs and other machines. There is a part called a power take-off. This has a spinning rod that works devices such as muck spreaders and hedge cutters.

LEVERS AND SWITCHES

The farmer works the tractor with levers and switches in the cab. The levers and switches also work the machinery the tractor is pulling.

SOME TRACTORS HAVE TRACKS LIKE A DIGGER INSTEAD OF WHEELS.

FORK-LIFT TRUCK

This big machine is called a fork-lift truck. It picks things up using two prongs that look like a fork. Fork-lift trucks work in factories. They move piles of heavy boxes and sacks around, loading them on to trucks.

TURNING TIGHTLY

Fork-lift trucks have to turn round in small spaces. The driver can turn the steering wheel with one hand, using the knob.

THE CHUNKY TIRES ARE FOR WORKING ON ROUGH GROUND.

HUGE FORK-LIFT TRUCKS 52 FEET LONG WERE USED TO LAY PIPES IN LIBYA.

DID YOU KNOW?

Objects that are moved by fork-lift trucks are piled on top of wooden trays called pallets. The pallets have slots underneath for the forks to fit into.

TELESCOPIC ARM

This big fork-lift truck has a telescopic arm. 'Telescopic' means that the arm can get longer or shorter. The arm can also lift up so the truck can pile boxes on top of each other and reach high shelves. The arm is moved by hydraulic rams.

A HINGE IN THE CENTER LETS THE TRUCK TURN CORNERS.

THIS IS THE TELESCOPIC ARM.

MANISCOPIC

THESE ARE THE FORKS THAT LIFT THINGS UP.

PICKING UP AND PUTTING DOWN

How does a fork-lift truck pick up a box? The driver puts the forks on the ground and drives forwards so that they slide under the box. The driver tips the forks backwards to stop the box sliding off, then drives away.

SOME FORK-LIFT TRUCKS CAN BE OPERATED BY REMOTE CONTROL!

THE MACHINE QUIZ

1. WHAT LUXURY ITEM DOES THE BIGGEST LIMOUSINE HAVE INSIDE?
a) Tennis court
b) Bowling alley
c) Swimming pool

2. WHAT DO FORMULA 1 DRIVERS SPRAY AT EACH OTHER AFTER THE END OF A RACE?
a) Lemonade
b) Water pistols
c) Champagne

3. HOW LONG DOES IT TAKE THE MACLAREN SPORTS CAR TO REACH 60 MPH?
a) Under 4 seconds
b) 2 minutes
c) Half an hour

4. WHAT IS A RICKSHAW?
a) An early motorbike
b) An armored car
c) A three-wheeled taxi

5. WHY DO 4 X 4 CARS HAVE BIG, GROOVED TIRES?
a) To allow them to ride over rough or muddy ground
b) To allow them to generate greater speed
c) To make sure they don't squash bugs underneath

6. VINTAGE CARS WERE MADE OUT OF METAL AND WHAT MATERIAL?
a) Plastic
b) Rubber
c) Wood

7. HOW MANY GEARS DOES A SMART CAR HAVE?
a) 0
b) 2
c) 5

8. HOW LONG IS THE BIGGEST HELICOPTER IN THE WORLD?
a) 66 feet
b) 98 feet
c) 132 feet

9. WHAT IS THE NAME GIVEN TO THE AERIAL STUNTS PERFORMED BY BIPLANE PILOTS?
a) Aeronautics
b) Aerobics
c) Aerobatics

10. WHAT IS THE NAME GIVEN TO A FIGHT BETWEEN TWO WARPLANES?
a) Catfight
b) Dogfight
c) Bullfight

11. WHY DO GLIDERS HAVE SEATBELTS FITTED?
a) It is against the law to fly without wearing a seatbelt
b) They stop the pilot falling out when the gliders go upside down
c) As a fashion statement

12. WHICH WERE THE FIRST CREATURES TO GO UP IN A HOT-AIR BALLOON?
a) A sheep, a rooster and a duck
b) One man and his dog
c) Three blind mice

13. WHICH IS THE FASTEST TYPE OF SMALL JET?
a) Lear Jet
b) Tear Jet
c) Fear Jet

14. WHAT IS THE NAME OF THE INFLATABLE LINING AROUND A HOVERCRAFT?
a) Rubber skirt
b) Rubber shirt
c) Plastic belt

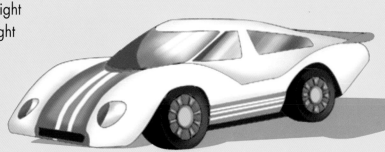

15. WHAT IS THE NAME GIVEN TO BOATS USED FOR PULLING OTHER SHIPS IN AND OUT OF HARBOR?

a) Heave

b) Tug

c) Push

16. WHAT IS THE NAME OF THE FASTEST TYPE OF RACING DINGHY?

a) Meringue

b) Catamaran

c) Cat-o'-nine-tails

17. HOW LONG WOULD IT TAKE THE FASTEST SPEEDBOAT TO TRAVEL DOWN THE NILE?

a) Half an hour

b) 13 hours

c) 2 days

18. WHY DO FISHING NETS HAVE HOLES IN THEM?

a) To let the water through

b) To let the baby fish escape

c) Because they haven't been made properly

19. WHERE IS FOOD PREPARED ON WARSHIPS?

a) Gallery

b) Museum

c) Galley

20. WHAT IS THE NAME GIVEN TO FERRIES THAT TAKE CARS BETWEEN TWO POINTS SEVERAL TIMES A DAY?

a) Roll-over

b) Turnover

c) Roll-on, Roll-off

21. WHAT IS THE NAME OF THE MACHINE THAT PULLS BROKEN-DOWN CARS ONTO A TOW TRUCK?

a) Winch

b) Pinch

c) Wench

22. WHAT DOES THE DRIVER OF A TRACTOR-TRAILER DO IF HE NEEDS TO VISIT THE LOO?

a) Cross his legs and wait for the next service station

b) Stop the truck and find the nearest sheltered spot

c) Visit the on-board toilet

23. WHAT KIND OF TRUCKS ARE USED TO CARRY LIQUID ABOUT?

a) Tonka truck

b) Banker truck

c) Tanker truck

24. HOW ARE TRUCKS MOVED FROM THE MANUFACTURERS TO THE SHOWROOMS?

a) On the back of tractors

b) They are towed by African elephants

c) On the back of other trucks

25. WHAT IS ON THE BACK OF SOME TRUCKS?

a) A conservatory

b) A lift

c) A swimming pool

26. HOW DO GARBAGE TRUCKS GET THE MOST GARBAGE POSSIBLE ON BOARD?

a) The garbage men stamp on the garbage until it is flat

b) The garbage trucks have crushers on board

c) They only take small bags

27. WHAT TYPE OF VANS ARE USED FOR CARRYING VALUABLES?

a) Camper vans

b) Monster vans

c) Armored vans

28. WHAT DID THE FIRST TRAINS RUN ON?

a) Diesel

b) Helium

c) Steam

29. HOW FAST DID THE FASTEST TGV TRAIN TRAVEL IN FRANCE IN 1990?

a) 93 mph

b) 195 mph

c) 320 mph

30. WHAT WOULD HAPPEN IF A TRAIN DRIVER LET GO OF THE LEVER USED TO CONTROL THE TRAIN?
a) The train would automatically stop
b) The train would derail
c) The train would go out of control

31. WHAT WERE THE FIRST TROLLEYS POWERED BY?
a) Donkeys
b) Horses
c) Electricity

32. WHO INVENTED THE DIESEL ENGINE?
a) Rudolf Petrol
b) Rudolf Diesel
c) Rudolf Gas-fired Turbine

33. WHICH TRAINS HAVE NO DRIVERS?
a) Ghost trains
b) Steam trains
c) Monorails

34. WHAT DO MINIATURE TRAINS RUN ON?
a) Wind-up motors
b) Ice cream and jello
c) Diesel

35. WHY DO FARMERS USE QUAD BIKES?
a) For racing each other around the fields
b) For taking food to sheep and cattle
c) To impress the local ladies

36. WHAT IS A MOTORBIKE TRIAL?
a) A test designed specially for trials bikes
b) A court case involving two motorbikes
c) A motorbike designed to test your patience

37. WITH WHAT DID GANGS OF SCOOTER RIDERS CUSTOMISE THEIR BIKES IN THE 1960S AND 70S?
a) Machine guns
b) On-board jukeboxes
c) Dozens of wing mirrors

38. WHAT IS A DRAG RACE?
a) A really boring race
b) A race between monster customised bikes
c) A race where the riders are dragged along behind the bikes

39. WHY WERE MOTORBIKE RACES BANNED FROM PUBLIC ROADS?
a) Because of the danger to pedestrians
b) Because the road surfaces weren't fast enough
c) Because the traffic got in the way

40. WHAT WERE EARLY MOTORCYCLES POWERED BY?
a) Horses
b) Steam
c) Wind

41. WHY DO SUPERBIKE RIDERS CROUCH DOWN WHILST RIDING?
a) Because the seats are so uncomfortable
b) To make the bikes go even faster
c) So they are not spotted by police cars

42. WHY DO POLICE CARS HAVE RADIOS INSIDE THEM?
a) They can't afford CD players
b) To keep up with the latest tunes
c) To correspond with the police station

43. HOW DO FIRE FIGHTERS REACH HIGH BLAZES?
a) By using a rising platform
b) By wearing platform heels
c) By standing on each other's shoulders when they are reversing

44. WHY IS THE WORD "AMBULANCE" WRITTEN BACKWARDS ON AN AMBULANCE?

a) Because the signwriter made a mistake

b) So drivers can read the word properly in rear view mirrors

c) So the word can be read properly when ambulances are reversing

45. WHAT HAPPENS IF A LIFEBOAT CAPSIZES?

a) It is rescued by an air-sea-rescue helicopter

b) The crew have to swim to shore

c) The boat won't sink – it has a self-righting mechanism

46. WHAT TYPE OF MOTORBIKE DO THE AMERICAN POLICE USE?

a) Jim Davidson

b) Harley Davidson

c) Peter Davidson

47. WHAT IS THE LADDER CALLED ON A LADDER TRUCK?

a) Microscopic ladder

b) Telescopic ladder

c) Semisonic ladder

48. WHAT IS THE OLDEST AIR-SEA-RESCUE ORGANISATION IN THE WORLD?

a) R.N.I.B.

b) R.S.P.C.A.

c) R.N.L.I.

49. WHAT MACHINE WOULD YOU USE TO MOVE A LOAD OF RUBBLE?

a) Digger

b) Glider

c) Loader

50. WHAT IS THE DIGGING MECHANISM CALLED IN A DIGGER?

a) Scoop

b) Bucket

C) Tub

51. HOW MANY CARS IS A MOBILE CRANE CAPABLE OF LIFTING?

a) 5

b) 30

c) 95

52. HOW DID THE FIRST FARMERS OPERATE PLOUGHS?

a) They were pulled by dinosaurs

b) They were pulled by horses

c) The farmers had to pull them themselves

53. WHAT HAS THE MOST POWERFUL ENGINE?

a) Superbike

b) Sports car

c) Combine harvester

54. WHAT REVOLUTIONARY NEW TRACTOR HAS JUST BEEN INVENTED?

a) A tractor that will do 124 mph

b) A tractor with an onboard bath and shower

c) A tractor that will plough a field by itself

55. HOW LONG ARE THE LONGEST FORK-LIFT TRUCKS IN THE WORLD?

a) 16 feet

b) 32 feet

c) 320 feet

ANSWERS

1 *c*), 2 *c*), 3 *a*), 4 *c*), 5 *a*), 6 *c*), 7 *b*), 8 *c*), 9 *c*), 10 *b*), 11 *b*), 12 *a*), 13 *a*), 14 *a*), 15 *b*), 16 *b*), 17 *b*), 18 *b*), 19 *c*), 20 *c*), 21 *a*), 22 *c*), 23 *c*), 24 *c*), 25 *b*), 26 *b*), 27 *c*), 28 *c*), 29 *c*), 30 *a*), 31 *c*), 32 *b*), 33 *c*), 34 *c*), 35 *b*), 36 *a*), 37 *c*), 38 *b*), 39 *a*) 40 *b*), 41 *b*), 42 *c*), 43 *a*), 44 *b*), 45 *c*), 46 *b*), 47 *b*), 48 *c*), 49 *a*), 50 *b*), 51 *b*), 52 *c*) 53 *c*), 54 *c*), 55 *c*).

INDEX

A

4 x 4s *18, 19, 80*

aerobatics *27*

air ambulances *99*

air-sea-rescue *106, 107*

aircraft *7, 24-37*

airliners *28, 29*

airports *97*

airships *35*

Alton Towers *78*

ambulances *8, 98, 99*

anchors *49*

armoured vans *65*

articulated lorries *54, 55*

Austin Seven *20, 21*

automatic trains *77*

B

backhoes *108*

balloons *34, 35*

battleships *48, 49*

bikes see motorbikes

biplanes *26, 27*

black cabs *16*

BMW *15*

boats *7, 8, 38-51*

Boeing 747 *29*

bombers *29*

brakes *91, 102, 111*

buffers *66, 74, 78*

builders *19*

Bumble Bee Two *36*

C

cables *51, 72*

Cadillac *11*

capsize *43, 101*

car carriers *58, 59*

cargo vans *64, 65*

cars *6, 10-23*

catamarans *42*

CB radios *54*

chains *82, 93*

Channel Tunnel *69*

chauffeurs *11*

chopper *86*

combine harvester *116, 117*

commuter trains *70, 71*

coupling *70*

cranes *60, 112, 113*

crushers *62*

custom bikes *86, 87*

D

diesel engines *53, 55, 75, 119*

diesel locomotives *74, 75*

Diesel, Rudolf *75*

diggers *110, 111*

dinghies *42, 43, 44, 45*

Disneyworld *77*

dogfights *31*

double-decker carriages *71*

drag racing *12, 87*

E

ejector seats *30*

electric cars *22*

electric motors *71, 72*

emergency vehicles *8, 94-107*

engines *91, 93, 95, 110, 116, 119*

    diesel *53, 55, 75, 119*

    jet *36, 49*

    motorbike *80*

    single cylinder *91*

    traction *118*

    turboprop *36, 37*

envelopes *34*

Eurostar *68*

F

farmers *8, 9, 19, 81*

Ferrari *13, 15*

ferries *38, 50, 51*

fighter bombers *31*

fighter planes *30, 31*

fire engines *60, 96, 97*

fire fighting *8, 41, 104*

fire-fighting tugs *41*

firemen, on steam locomotives *67*

fishing boats *46, 47*

flat trucks *60*

floating mobile cranes *113*

floats *60*

Florida *77*

fork-lift trucks *120, 121*

forks *82, 86*

Formula 1 racing cars *14*

four-wheel drive *18, 19*

France *69*

freight trains *74*

funnels **67**

furrows **115**

fuselage **26**

G

garbage (rubbish) trucks **60**

gas **56**

Germany **76**

gliders **32, 33**

guided missiles **49**

guns **31, 49**

H

hang-gliders **33**

Harley Davidson **87, 102**

hedge cutters **119**

helicopters **10, 24, 25, 48**

    rescue **8, 24, 99, 100, 106, 107**

high-speed trains **68, 69**

Honda **92**

horse-trams **73**

horses **96, 114, 117**

hoses **96, 97**

hot-air balloons **34, 35**

hovercraft **38, 39**

hydraulic rams **58**

hydrofoils **39**

I

inshore fishing boats **47**

Isle of Man **73**

J

Japan **68, 70**

Jeep **19**

jet airliners **28, 29**

jet engines **36, 49**

L

ladder trucks **104, 105**

Lamborghini **15**

Lear jets **37**

Libya **120**

lifeboats **100, 101, 107**

lifting machinery **63**

light aircraft **36, 37**

limousines **10, 11**

Lincoln **11**

loaders **108, 109**

loading, trucks **61**

lobster pots **47**

locomotives

    diesel **74, 75**

    steam **66, 67, 78, 79**

looping the loop **27**

M

Maclaren **14**

maglev trains **76**

magnetic trains **68, 76**

Mallard (steam locomotive) **67**

Mercedes Benz **11**

mini diggers **111**

mini-buses **64**

miniature trains **78, 79**

missiles **31, 49**

mobile cranes **60, 112, 113**

model steam locomotives **78**

Model-T Ford **20**

mods **85**

monorail trains **76, 77**

motor boats **44, 45**

motorbike engines **80**

motorbike trials **83**

motorbikes **8, 80-93**

    custom **86, 87**

    police patrol **102, 103**

    quad **8, 80, 81**

    racing **8, 12, 81, 87, 88, 89**

    superbikes **92, 93**

    trials **82, 83**

    vintages **90, 91**

motorized dinghies **45**

mountain rescue **107**

muck spreaders **119**

mudguards **81, 82**

O

oil power **108**

outboard motors 44

P

pallets **121**

panel vans **64**

pantographs **69**

paragliders **32**

paramedics **98, 99**

pick-up trucks **52, 53**

pits **13**

ploughs **114, 115**

police **8, 57**

patrol bikes **102, 103**

patrol cars **94, 95**

Porsche **15**

portholes **50**

powders, carried by tankers **57**

powerboats **44**

propeller airliner **37**

Q

quad bikes **8, 80, 81**

R

racing bikes **8, 88, 89**

racing cars **12, 13**

racing trucks **55**

radar **101**

radio **94, 98, 100, 103**

rallies **20, 83, 90**

rams **108, 110, 111, 121**

recovery trucks **52, 53**

recycling **63**

refrigerated units **61**

rescue **45**

air-sea **106, 107**

helicopters **8, 24, 99, 100, 106, 107**

mountain **107**

trucks **9**

rickshaws **16**

rigid trucks **60, 61**

R.N.L.I. **107**

road trains **54**

rockets **31**

roll-on roll-off ferries **50, 51**

rotors **24, 25, 106**

rubber dinghies **45**

rubbish (garbage) trucks **9, 60, 62, 63**

rubble moving **108**

S

sailing dinghies **42, 43**

salvage tugs **40**

San Francisco **72**

scooters **84, 85, 87**

scuppers **46**

self-righting lifeboats **101**

ships **48, 49, 101**

shunting locomotives **74, 75**

single cylinder engines **91**

Smart cars **22, 23**

sonar machines **47**

speedway races **89**

sports cars **14, 15**

steam locomotives **66, 67, 78, 79**

steam trains **66, 67, 78, 79**

super ferries **50**

superbikes **92, 93**

Sydney **76, 77**

T

tankers **56, 57, 60**

taxis **16, 17**

telescopic arms **121**

TGV trains **69**

three-wheeled custom bikes **86**

torpedoes **49**

tow trucks **52, 53**

tracks **110, 119**

traction engines **118**

tractor units **54, 55**

tractors **9, 114, 115, 118, 119**

trailers **54**

train ferries **51**

trains **6, 58, 66, 66-79, 67**

automatic **77**

commuter **70, 71**

freight **74**

high-speed **68, 69**

maglev **76**

magnetic **68, 76**

miniature **78 79**

monorail **76, 77**

road **54**

steam **66, 67, 7, 9**

TGV **69**

underground **70**

trams **72, 73**

trials bikes **82, 83**

truck racing **55**

trucks **9, 52-65, 104, 105, 120, 121**

flat **60**

fork-lift **120, 121**

garbage (rubbish) **9, 60, 62, 63**

ladder **104, 105**

pick-up **52, 53**

recovery **52, 53**

rescue **9**

rigid **60, 61**

rubbish (garbage) **9, 60, 62, 63**

tow **52, 53**

tugs **40, 41**

turboprop engines **36, 37**

turntable ladders **105**

tyres **82, 89, 93, 119**

U

underground trains **70**

U.S.A. **74, 102**

V

vans **9, 64, 65, 94**

ventilation **69**

vintage cars **20, 21**

vintage motorbikes **90, 91**

W

warning signs **56**

water tankers **56**

wheelies **93**

Williams **13**

winches **52, 106**

working vehicles **9, 108-21**